Practical Graph Structures in SQL Server and Azure SQL

Enabling Deeper Insights Using Highly Connected Data

Louis Davidson

Apress®

Practical Graph Structures in SQL Server and Azure SQL: Enabling Deeper Insights Using Highly Connected Data

Louis Davidson
Cleveland, TN, USA

ISBN-13 (pbk): 978-1-4842-9458-1
https://doi.org/10.1007/978-1-4842-9459-8

ISBN-13 (electronic): 978-1-4842-9459-8

Managing Director, Apress Media LLC: Welmoed Spahr
Acquisitions Editor: Jonathan Gennick
Development Editor: Laura Berendson
Editorial Project Manager: Shaul Elson
Copy Editor: Mary Behr

Cover image by Garry Killian from Freepik (www.freepik.com)

Distributed to the book trade worldwide by Springer Science+Business Media LLC, 1 New York Plaza, Suite 4600, New York, NY 10004. Phone 1-800-SPRINGER, fax (201) 348-4505, e-mail orders-ny@springer-sbm. com, or visit www.springeronline.com. Apress Media, LLC is a California LLC and the sole member (owner) is Springer Science + Business Media Finance Inc (SSBM Finance Inc). SSBM Finance Inc is a **Delaware** corporation.

For information on translations, please e-mail booktranslations@springernature.com; for reprint, paperback, or audio rights, please e-mail bookpermissions@springernature.com.

Apress titles may be purchased in bulk for academic, corporate, or promotional use. eBook versions and licenses are also available for most titles. For more information, reference our Print and eBook Bulk Sales web page at www.apress.com/bulk-sales.

Any source code or other supplementary material referenced by the author in this book is available to readers on GitHub (https://github.com/Apress). For more detailed information, please visit www.apress. com/source-code.

Printed on acid-free paper

To Val, what a life we have had so far... here's to more of it.

Table of Contents

About the Author ix

About the Technical Reviewer xi

Acknowledgments xiii

Preface xv

Chapter 1: Introduction to Graphs 1

Graph Fundamentals.. 3

Definition 4

Summary.. 15

Chapter 2: Data Structures and Algorithms... 17

Basic Implementation 17

Acyclic Graphs 19

Trees... 22

Other Acyclic Graphs 27

Cyclic Graphs 30

Non-Directed Graphs 35

Summary.. 36

Chapter 3: SQL Graph Table Basics... 39

Object Creation 40

Creating Data 43

Querying Data 48

Node-to-Node Querying... 48

Traversing Variable Level Paths... 59

Summary.. 75

Chapter 4: SQL Graph Tables: Extended Topics.................................... **77**

Advanced Data Creation Techniques.. 77

    Building an Interface Layer.. 78

    Loading Data Using Composable JSON Tags.................................... 87

Heterogenous Queries... 93

Integrity Constraints and Indexes 101

    Edge Constraint 101

    Uniqueness Constraints (and Indexes) 107

    Additional Constraints 111

Metadata Roundup... 115

    List Graph Objects in the Database 115

    Types of Graph Columns.. 116

    Tools for Fetching Graph Information 117

Summary... 118

Chapter 5: Tree Data Structures **121**

Creating the Data Structures 122

    Base Table Structures.. 122

    Demo Sales Structure.. 125

Essential Tree Maintenance Code 127

    Code To Create New Nodes 128

    Reparenting Nodes 138

    Deleting a Node 141

Tree Output Code.. 148

    Returning Part of the Tree.. 149

    Determining If a Child Node Exists 151

    Aggregating Child Activity at Every Level 154

Summary... 162

Chapter 6: Tree Structures, Algorithms, and Performance **163**

Alternative Tree Implementation 164

    Path Technique 166

    Helper Table.. 175

Performance Comparison 186

Summary... 189

Chapter 7: Other Directed Acyclic Graphs **191**

The Problem Set.. 191

The Example 193

Determining If a Part Is Used in a Build 197

Picking Items for a Build 200

Printing Out the Parts List for a Build.. 201

Summary... 206

Chapter 8: A Graph For Testing **209**

The Example 209

    Creating the Tables... 210

    Loading the Data 212

    The Queries 215

Performance Tuning Results 228

Performance Tuning Roundup.. 231

    Test.. 231

    Index the Internal Columns.. 231

    Employ a Maximum Degree of Parallelism of One 232

    Consider Breaking Up Some Queries.. 232

The End (or Is It the Beginning?)... 233

Index... **235**

About the Author

 **Louis Davidson** has been working with databases for more than 25 years as a corporate database developer and architect. He is now the editor for the Redgate Simple Talk website. He has been a Microsoft MVP for 18 years. In addition to this book on graphs in SQL Server, he has written six editions of his general-purpose SQL Server database design book (Apress) and has worked on multiple other book projects over the years.

Louis has been active in speaking about database design and implementation at many conferences over the past 25 years, including SQL PASS, SQL Rally, SQL Saturday events, CA World, Music City Data, and the devLink Technical Conference. He has a bachelor's degree in computer science from the University of Tennessee at Chattanooga. For more information, please visit his website at drsql.org.

About the Technical Reviewer

**Kathi Kellenberger** is a Customer Success Engineer at Redgate and a Data Platform MVP. She has worked with SQL Server since 1998 and has authored, co-authored, or tech reviewed over 20 technical books. Kathi is a longtime volunteer at LaunchCode in St. Louis where she has taught T-SQL in the LaunchCode Women + program. When Kathi isn't working, she enjoys spending time with family and friends, cycling, singing, and climbing the stairs of tall buildings.

Acknowledgments

My wife, for suffering through yet another long and painful book writing process.

The Microsoft MVP Program for all the connections it has provided me to meet wonderful, bizarrely smart people for 18 years. And my lead, Rie Merritt, for all she has done for me through the years; amazing how we met so many years ago. Just meeting Bob Ward and Conor Cunningham is thrill enough, and there have been hundreds besides them.

Shreya Verma and Arvind Shyamsundar for their help over the past few years as I attempted to do crazy things with the graph objects on my local personal computer.

Dr. David Rosenstein, who first got me interested in graphs in relational structures so many years ago. Paul Nielsen for the talks we had on graph structures.

Kathi Kellenberger for tech editing this book. I appreciate the hard work!

All the doctors/medical professionals who kept me alive and kicking these past few years. (If you want to know more, just ask, if you have a while to talk. There is a reason this book took me over two years to write.)

My coworkers at CBN whom I left during the writing of this book. I hope the graph objects I left you with are serving you nicely.

My new coworkers at Redgate. I have been a friend of Redgate (as well as a member of Friends of Redgate) for many years, writing for them. My new manager and teammates have been nothing but awesome.

Amber Davis, for giving me the chance to be a Dollywood Insider. Obviously being a Dollywood insider has little to do with this book, but I just wanted to say it again (which she may never see!) as I am writing the acknowledgements in the Dollywood Dreammore lobby. I learned a lot from her that has been useful writing some of this book and in my new job at Redgate as Simple-Talk editor.

Preface

I started working on my first book 23 years ago. It was on relational database design. I had learned a little about graphs at that point from a class I took by Dr. David Rozenshtein (his 1997 book *The Essence of SQL : A Guide to Learning Most of SQL in the Least Amount of Time* was essential). His class was very influential and taught me a lot about how to think about SQL problems. This was a really long time ago (clearly), but in that same class, one of the sections was on trees in SQL Server. I was hooked on the subject.

In my 2012 edition of my database design book, I started to include hierarchies as one of the topics. In my latest book, that came out after SQL Server 2019 arrived, I promised a book of SQL Graph. This book in your hands is the answer to that challenge.

This is my first programming-based book in many years. Usually I am more interested in helping you shape a design, but in this case, I want to show you the mechanics of building a graph database solution using SQL Server and leave it more to you to decide what to do with it from there. Part of this is due to the newness and relative complexity of the topic, but also because graphs are meant to be very flexible structures…way more flexible than the standard relational databases.

The chapters of the book are as follows:

- Chapter 1: What a graph is and ways graphs can be used. I touch on some of the underpinnings of what makes a graph a graph and a taste of the theory that mathematicians use to describe and work with graph data structures.

- Chapter 2: How graphs are implemented and the algorithms that are used to process them. While the basic structure of the graph is really simple, there is some value to understanding how graph structures are built in coding and having some idea of what you will see in the rest of the book.

- Chapter 3: The syntax that Microsoft has implemented for use with graph data stored in SQL Server tables is similar to what you probably already know from working with relational tables, but it is so much more. In this chapter, I teach you how to use the syntax provided by Microsoft to query graph tables in interesting ways.

- Chapter 4: Whereas in Chapter 3 I showed basic query techniques, in this chapter I show methods that can help you load and protect the integrity of the data in your SQL Graph tables.

- Chapter 5: A tree structure built using SQL Graph objects, including code to load and manipulate those nodes in ways that you will need when building production systems. In this chapter, you explore the code to create and manage a tree in SQL Server, along with an example of how it all works.

- Chapter 6: In this chapter, I dig into performance. You'll examine a new method of implementing a tree for comparison to the SQL Graph objects and build some objects you can use to write queries to report on data in your trees that operate faster. You will then build some large, random data sets and compare how these methods perform with certain larger sized data sets.

- Chapter 7: The goal of this chapter is to build a data structure that can show some of the concerns with working with directed graphs that are not trees. You will build a fairly simple bill of materials data structure to demonstrate the techniques you will need when you are working with these structures, which are similar to trees but still quite different.

- Chapter 8: In this chapter, you will do some querying of larger data sets in SQL Server's graph objects. To do this, you will implement a graph structure and data generation tools to try on large sets of data to match your expected needs. Finally, you will explore a set of performance tips for handling graph objects.

SQL Server's relational engine may never be acceptable as a complete replacement for a specific graph database system like CosmosDB, but even in its relative infancy with just a few iterations complete in the SQL Server lifecycle, it has become a nice way to extend your data structures inside existing relational data structures quickly and easily.

You can find the downloads in the book in two locations. First, on Apress's website you will find the original code for this book and any errata that is reported: `https://github.com/Apress/practical-graph-structures`. Second, at `https://github.com/drsqlgithub/GraphBook1` you will find that code plus any new code and projects I create that pertain to learning graphs until I start working on a second edition of this book someday.

If you have any direct questions about the content, send email to `louis@drsql.org` and I will do what I can.

CHAPTER 1

Introduction to Graphs

With great power comes great responsibility.

--Voltaire (and Spider-Man's Uncle Ben)

At its core, a graph data structure is simply a model representing the connection of one thing to one other thing and then those things to even more other things. Essentially a graph database formalizes a database based on many-to-many relationships as the core relationship.

Everyone who has ever modeled a relational database will either have modeled a graph purposefully or inadvertently because many-to-many relationships begin to appear as you add more concepts to your data model. The vast difference you will see is that relational implementations, ideally, are rigidly modeled.

The term frequently used to decide whether to model a many-to-many relationship in a relational database or a graph structure is whether the data is **highly connected**. With a graph database structure, you can connect many tables to many other tables and query that structure in a different (yet quite similar) manner to how you query a relational database.

There are many examples of graphs, but some of the most common examples you probably hear about are

- Social networks, where you record the relationship from one person to another

- Suggestion processing systems like online retailers use to record the relationship between a person and the products they have looked at and ordered and how that matches up with other people who have similar interests

- Manager-employee relationships where the employee has a manager who also has a manager who is likely managed by someone else

© Louis Davidson 2023
L. Davidson, *Practical Graph Structures in SQL Server and Azure SQL*,
https://doi.org/10.1007/978-1-4842-9459-8_1

With this information, you can discover interesting things about an object based on its relationships and similarity to relationships other entities have.

Possibly the most famous graph that most people will have heard of is the basis of the parlor game "Six Degrees of Kevin Bacon." This game suggests that everyone is no more than six connections away from anyone else, including Kevin Bacon (and not just that your favorite breakfast meat is bacon.)

The fact that graphs are very natural data structures does not make them easy to work with. Because they are less rigid data structures than relational tables, the flexibility makes them quite complex to work with (certainly in the database engine). Graph objects can represent a very messy reality, and the more complex the data you are modeling, the more complicated it is to work with. Of course, the reward for that complexity is the solutions you create are often quite tremendous.

Like many computer science topics, graphs are also a fundamental mathematical concept. Some of the insights you can get from the math of graphs will help once we start analyzing data. So, to begin this book on graphs, I will provide a very cursory look at some mathematical concepts as I define what a graph is and how it can be used in software.

Note that the concepts in this chapter were gleaned from many resources and are generally common knowledge. However, when I was searching for resources to read for an introduction to the concepts of graphs, including mathematical proofs (none of which will come up in this book, so no worries!) of such concepts, one was *Introduction to Graph Theory* by Richard J. Trudeau from Dover Publications in 1993. It is far deeper than this chapter and definitely more than you need to learn to code with SQL Server's graph database extensions, and mathematical proofs have always been my Kryptonite! However, I highly recommend this as a place to ascend to the next level beyond what I will show you.

This chapter will be a quick, high-level overview of the many topics you will find in this book and many other sources, plus ideas you may wish to use in the graph table objects I will cover once you start building objects. The book itself will be mostly focused on very practical applications and how to write certain types of code, but I found that knowing some of the graph fundamentals really helped me to envision what I was attempting to accomplish.

Graph Fundamentals

While most readers will have the explicit goal of applying a graph to a specific problem they are trying to solve, it is best to start at the beginning and discuss what a graph is in the pure sense. (If you don't care, you can skip to Chapter 3 where the T-SQL code starts!) Going through the fundamentals will help you free your mind from preconceived notions. Perhaps, more importantly, you can ignore the limitations of the tools and specific problem sets you may wish to solve and just think about the whole problem set.

In math, there are the concepts of "pure" math and "applied" math. Pure math is math for math's sake. It is there to ask, "what can be done with a construct?" without asking the limiting questions of, "is this helpful code to solve my problem or, even more importantly, any problem?" Applied math is more or less the sort of thing we typical computer architects/programmers are typically interested in since we have a problem and want to find something to help us with that problem (and immediately so). Most of the time, solutions are only interesting if they can solve the specific problems we currently know about and have a manager riding on our back.

However, I always prefer to start just trying to see what I can accomplish with a new tool before getting my hands dirty (metaphorically, of course; as a programmer, my hands never get dirty at work unless the day's snack includes chocolate).

Some of the things I will discuss will then be familiar in understanding what we might do when looking for patterns in the data and eventually translating into algorithms. Some designs may not be realistically possible due to current computing limitations in SQL Server (or any graph database platform) or reasonable hardware limitations at the time of writing in 2023. Having written my first book in 2000, it astounds me how different this statement feels to me 23 years later sitting here with a computer on my desk that has more power that medium to large corporations were running on when I first wrote T-SQL.

In one of my sample databases you can download, I have millions of rows in just one table, and I can process reasonable queries on my desktop computer in mere minutes. Limitations always exist, but there are fewer and fewer limitations for every generation of computer architecture that passes.

My goal here in this first chapter (and to a large extent, the second chapter) is to simply introduce some of the terms and concepts around graphs to help you understand how graphs are shaped and, eventually, processed.

Definition

Graphs are based on two primary data structures: **nodes** (or in math terms, vertices), and **edges**. Nodes represent a *thing* that one might care about, much like a table in a relational database. Edges establish a connection between exactly one or two nodes (when the node count is one, it means the node is related to itself.) A graph is defined as being a set of nodes and a set of edges.

In a graph database, a node is like most any table with attributes describing what the node represents. The edge is analogous to a many-to-many relationship table with at least attributes to represent the node that the relationship is **from** and which it is **to**. You will see that two major things set these new concepts apart from a relational implementation.

First, the from and the to in an edge generally can be from any node object. Whereas a relational table column used to reference another table value communicates that it is a foreign key from Table X and nothing else, the from and to attributes of an edge can be from multiple different node types if you so desire.

Tip   I am fully aware that you *can* put any value into a column, so every foreign key value in a column needn't come from the same table. But that is not how it *should* be done because data where a column can mean multiple things is very confusing in a relational table. Graph structures work very similar to how relational tables work. Still, they have special properties that allow two rows to contain data from multiple sources without confusing the user/engine.

Second, to make use of these flexible structures, a special set of operations is enabled in a graph engine, allowing easier access to the meaning of the relationships than we can get using SQL. More detail on these operations and the basic algorithms are in Chapters 2 and 3.

For the first example, consider the simple graph represented in Figure 1-1—two nodes connected by a single edge. If the type of node is important, it will be indicated using different shapes.

Figure 1-1. Simple graph

When diagraming a graph, edges may also have a property of direction. The direction indicates that the relationship is not reciprocal. For example, consider Figure 1-2.

Figure 1-2. Simple directed graph

In this graph, N1 connects to N2, but N2 is not connected to N1. This is analogous to a social media relationship such as when I follow Paul McCartney, but Paul McCartney doesn't follow me! It will often be very important to understand the value of the direction because of the unbalanced nature of some relationships. Mr. McCartney doesn't all of the sudden wish to get any communication about where I am speaking at a conference, but I wish to be informed of his concerts and new music being released.

In SQL Graph, and other graph products, edges are almost always directed. This will become important later but will only complicate our discussion of graphs concepts in general, so to start with, let's ignore the directedness of the edges.

In my first example graph in Figure 1-1, I have two nodes and a single edge. This is a very simple graph, but it is not the simplest graph. The simplest graph is a graph with 0 edges and 0 nodes, otherwise referred to as the **NULL graph**. You can also have a graph with a single node and no edges, and a single node with a single edge, and so on. (You can't have an edge without a node.)

Just like modeling a relational database, there is an inherent danger in thinking of a graph as a drawing and not a complex data structure. Consider a graph with the nodes and edges seen in Figure 1-3.

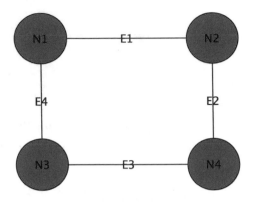

Figure 1-3. *Graph with four edges and four nodes*

This graph could be expressed as sets of nodes and edges in the following manner:

Nodes: {N1,N2,N3,N4}; Edges: {E1:{N1,N2}; E2:{N2,N4}; E3:{N3,N4}; E4:{N1,N3}}

By definition, all nodes and edges must be distinct, much like a table requires distinct rows. And just like a table, the order of the items in the sets has no importance. The following graph is the same as diagrammed and as defined prior to this paragraph:

Nodes: {N2,N3,N1,N4}; Edges: {E2:{N2,N4}; E1:{N1,N2}; E4:{N1,N3}; E3:{N3,N4}}

When drawing a graph as an image, there is a very similar consideration. Every programmer with any skill has frequented a white board to draw a diagram of a structure. If you were to draw a shape of a circle, a triangle, and a square on the white board, instinctively you would believe them to be different things. Even if you drew a rectangle, square, and a rhombus (all shapes with four sides) you would not think they were the same.

But, in graph terms (just like when diagramming tables), the two graphs in Figure 1-4 are the same as each other and the graph in Figure 1-3, in which they are considered "equal."

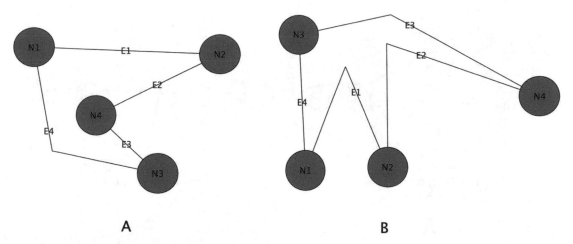

Figure 1-4. *Two identical graph structures*

The two graph diagrams in Figure 1-4 are copies of the same graph. The next concept is related, in that we will look at graphs with the same shape but different nodes. When a graph has the same node and edge shape (meaning the same nodes and edges, not diagram shape,) the graphs are referred to as being **isomorphic graphs**. For example, the two graphs in Figure 1-5 are not equal but they are isomorphic because they have the same shape in their set of data (regardless of whether you draw them as a square or not).

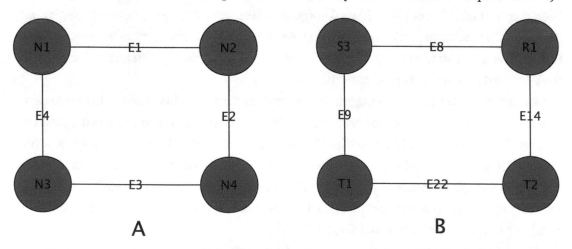

Figure 1-5. *Two isomorphic graph structures*

This concept of isomorphism will be, if not actually referred to using the exact term, interesting in your usage of graphs on occasion. Consider the set of nodes in Figure 1-6.

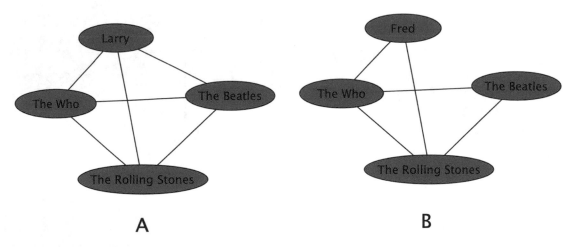

Figure 1-6. *Sample graphs for comparison*

Now, consider that the nodes {Larry, The Who, Rolling Stones}, which form what is known as a **subgraph** (a set of nodes and edges that is a part of a graph) of the more complete graph, are isomorphic to {Fred, The Who, Rolling Stones}. It isn't a difficult leap to see that since Fred and Larry are both connected to two similar nodes, that an additional edge {Fred, Beatles} might be a possibility for Fred. So, the company may then wish to suggest "Have you heard of The Beatles (or do you live under a rock)?" Of course, Fred may not be a fan of John, Paul, George, and Ringo; but the goal of many graphs may be to look for common traits and then suggest ways to make them more common. Take this further and you may see patterns occurring from completely different subgraphs that may indicate a repeatable pattern.

An important concept in subgraphs is a **walk** in a graph. This refers to how you can traverse from node to node. For example, in the first graph in Figure 1-6, starting at Larry you can find a walk from Larry -> TheWho -> Rolling Stones -> Beatles -> Larry. You can also find many other walks from any node to any node in this sample graph, since every node in the graph is connected to every other node. Another term for a walk is a **path**, which may be a bit more common since the operator you will use in SQL Server 2019 and later to find a walk is named SHORTEST_PATH.

You will often use this concept of a walk to determine the closest one node is to another. For example, in the second variant of the graph, the distance from Fred to The Who and Rolling Stones is 1 and to the Beatles is 2. If you are a user of LinkedIn, you have seen this concept when you see that you are a first-level connection or second or more to other people. A second-level connection means you are connected through one intermediate node.

A concept that is interesting if likely not particularly necessary in programming typical graph structures is a Euler (pronounced Oiler) Walk. An Euler Walk consists of the starting node being touched twice and every edge in the graph touched exactly once. For example, consider the graphs in Figure 1-7.

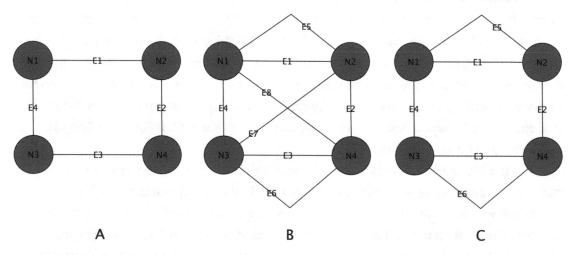

A   B   C

Figure 1-7. *Graph diagrams to demonstrate walks*

Note   This gets a little hard to express in text!

In Figure 1-7A, you can traverse from N1 back to N1 through E1->N2->E2->N4->E3->N3->E4. And in 1-7B, you can go starting and ending at N1, through E1->N2->E5->N1->E4->N3->E6->E3->N3->E7->N2->E2->N4->E8. However, in 1-7C, it is impossible to do this, because if you start at N1 and start a walk such as N1->E1->N2->E5->N1->E4, you will never be able to return to N1. It turns out that for a graph to have a Euler Walk, all the nodes must be of an even **degree** (the degree of a node indicates the number of edges connected to the node).

Note   A graph such as 1-7B and 1-7C is a **multigraph**. A multigraph allows that we have more than one edge between the same two nodes. As we get more complex, we can see that an edge often indicates a role that the nodes play in a relationship. Some edges don't make sense, having multiple edges between the same node; others may make perfect sense. Remember I said earlier that edges between nodes must be unique. These edges may not be equal, but instead say

---

two things about the relationship between to nodes, like in Figure 1-7b, N1->N2 has E1 and E5. One may be a familial relationship, the other a social network connection, which you probably would not want to be the same edge for the reason of traversing a specific type of edge.

Realistically the limitation will come down to the thing that all modeling decisions come to: *semantics*. What does the relationship mean and how will it be used to mean one or more relationships? For example, you might only logically have one edge between persons indicating that person is a biological parent to a person; on the other hand, multiple edges between person and movie could make sense: one for actor, one for producer, one for director, and so on.

One last bit of graph theory I want to cover is that of a **connected** graph. In a connected graph, there is a walk from every node in the graph to every other node. The graph will be in one or more pieces in a **disconnected graph**. In Figure 1-8, we have the simplest connected graph with more than one node in 1-8A and the simplest disconnected graph in 1-8B. The graph in 1-8A is said to be in one piece, and the graph in 1-8B is in two pieces.

Figure 1-8. *Simple connected and disconnected graphs*

In Figure 1-9, we have a more complex graph in three **pieces**.

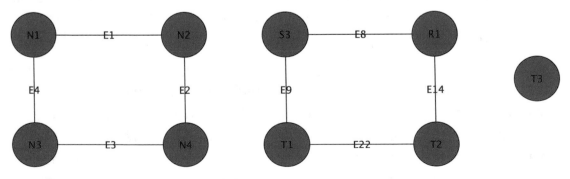

Figure 1-9. *Single graph in three pieces*

When you have a connected graphs and removing an edge will cause it to be broken into more pieces, the edge is referred to as a **bridge edge**. Consider the graph in Figure 1-10.

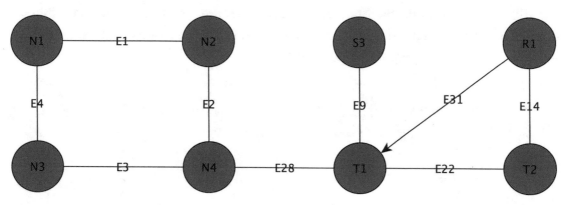

Figure 1-10. *Graph to demonstrate bridge edges*

There are two bridge edges in this graph. The most obvious is E28. If you remove it, you will have two multi-node pieces remaining. The one that is perhaps less obvious is E9. Removing E9 would leave S3 alone and hence one more piece to the graph. When the degree of a node is 2, removing any edge will leave the remaining edge a bridge edge.

Graphs In Computing/Directed Graphs

Now that I have introduced a subset of the terminology and shapes of graphs, it is time move towards the mechanics of graphs you will be building and using with SQL Server's SQL Graph feature (or really any mainstream graph product). All the aforementioned concepts still hold, but there is one major difference. Edges in computing terms are generally one way only. An edge that points in one direction only is referred to as a **directed edge** and the whole graph as a **directed graph**. I will not redefine all the previously introduced concepts in terms of directed graphs, as the goal of covering the topics was to get you thinking about graph structures and how they fit together. I will discuss how they are applicable as it makes sense.

Relationships in a directed graph are in the form shown in Figure 1-11.

Figure 1-11. *Directed edge*

Whereas in previous graph examples an edge between N1 and N2 represented that N1 was connected to N2 and N2 connected to N1, now edge E1 represents only that N1 is connected to N2, not the reciprocal. All the concepts covered previously hold, with the obvious complication that one must consider the direction of the edge when determining if two graphs are equal or isometric and what walks may be present. For example, consider the graphs in Figure 1-12.

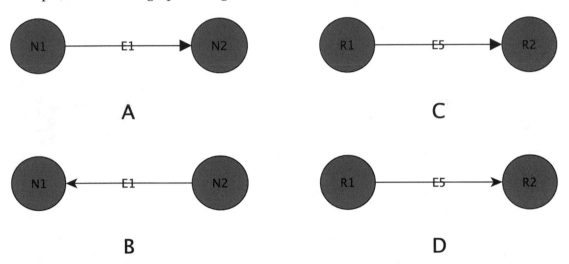

Figure 1-12. *Graph examples to demonstrate equality and isomorphism with a directed graph*

1-12A and 1-12B are not equal, but 1-12B is isometric because the edge is in a different direction, but the basic structure is two nodes connected by a directed edge.

1-12A and 1-12D are also not equal because the nodes are different, but they are isometric because structurally they are the same. 1-12C and 1-12D are exactly alike so they are equal.

When specifying a directed graph, you still can use the same set notation, except that you need to denote an ordering to the nodes. So, Figure 1-12A could be expressed as

Nodes: {N1,N2}; Directed Edges: {E1:{N1,N2}}

You can simulate the bidirectional qualities of a non-directed graph by always having two edges between each node:

Nodes: {N1,N2}; Directed Edges: {E1:{N1,N2}, E2:{N2,N1}}

Cyclic and Acyclic Graphs

With directed graphs comes a very important concept that will play a major part in of all our uses of graphs in practice: **cycles**. A graph cycle refers to a directional graph having a walk from a given node that can pass through the same node twice. It is similar to the concept of a Euler Walk, but in this case you can only traverse the graph based on the direction of the edges.

For examples, the simplest cyclical graph is a single node with a relationship to the same node, and the next simplest is two nodes and two edges going from and to each edge, as in Figure 1-13.

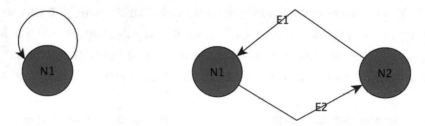

Figure 1-13. *Cyclic graph examples*

This concept of cyclical graphs is important for a couple of reasons. First, let's consider the programming concerns. Some algorithms will work great on acyclic graphs but will not work on cyclic graphs. The biggest issue is in processing. Consider the two graphs in Figure 1-14.

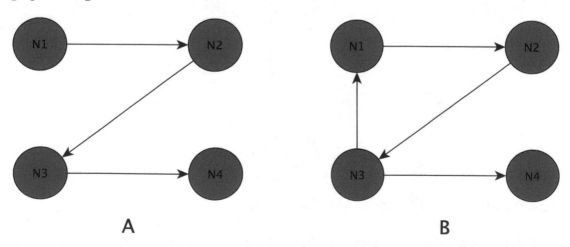

A   B

Figure 1-14. *Graph examples to demonstrate processing acyclic and cyclic directed graph*

13

In Figure 1-14A, an acyclic graph, you can walk the graph from N1->N2->N3->N4 directly using a simple algorithm of going node to node, touching all the nodes with no problem. But in Figure 1-14B, the algorithm of going from node to node is made difficult by N1->N2->N3->N1, because what to do next? Cycle through the nodes again? Or stop processing? All the results from starting at N1 would be repeated, but what does this mean for the graph that you are modeling? You can remember this mentally when manually tracing through, but the programming gets more complex if you look at millions or billions of nodes (the programming is not impossible, just more complicated).

This ability to be able to find a simple connection/walk from two nodes in a graph is referred to as **transitive closure**. Once you have hold of this power, you can do all forms of interesting things with graphs, such as determining if you are connected to Kevin Bacon and what is the shortest path through the people you are connected to that you will need to bug to get tickets to see The Bacon Brothers in concert when they come to your town.

In a more database design-oriented concern, consider what can be modeled with an acyclic graph versus a cyclic one. More will be covered in Chapter 2, but if you are modeling containership, like a bill of materials (a data structure used in packaging/assembling items, where products that are a part of other products are modeled using a graph), a cycle in the graph could give you odd results. Consider the graph in Figure 1-15.

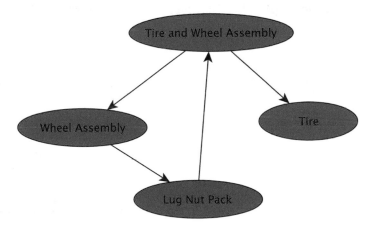

Figure 1-15. *Illogically modelled bill of materials*

If the tire and wheel assembly contains a wheel assembly, and it in turn contains lug nuts, and then the lug nuts contain a tire and wheel assembly... you can see the inherent problem here. If you are modeling something like a social network, cycles not only make sense, but you can find important information from them (starting with a simple reciprocal relationship showing that two people are connected.) In Chapter 2, I will be discussing some of the different constructs you can model using graph structures.

Acyclic graphs such as this are generally referred to as a class of data structures known as a hierarchy. In the case of the bill of materials structure, it is known as a **polyhierarchy**. A node in a polyhierarchy may be the "to" partner in more than one edge, but the graph must be acyclic. In this manner, one can think of the lug nut pack as a separate item or as a part of the wheel (and in the real world, the lug nut would be its own individual part!) but a lug nut pack cannot have the wheel or wheel assembly as part of its part list for obvious reasons.

Summary

In this chapter, the goal was to introduce some of the core concepts that are used when discussing graph topics. Many of these topics may show up all over the book, but also some may not. The goal of this chapter was to briefly introduce concepts that will help you to envision what a graph is and how a graph might be used as you start to solve complex problems with graphs.

CHAPTER 2

Data Structures and Algorithms

In this chapter, I will introduce the common graph configurations you can create using objects in SQL Server. I will start by defining the basics of how almost every graph structure is stored in a relational (or really, any) database. Creating the tables to hold the graph structures is quite straightforward; it is the processing of the data where things start to get complicated.

For each of the data structure configurations I will cover, I will include a high-level explanation of the algorithms you will use to process them. This will leave later chapters to simply build the code to process the data in the data structures.

Basic Implementation

As discussed in the previous chapter, the basic building blocks of a graph are nodes and edges. A node is basically the same thing as any relational database table representing some specific concept. An edge represents a link between two rows in these tables, much like a typical many-to-many resolution table does in a relational database.

So, say you have the graph shown in Figure 2-1.

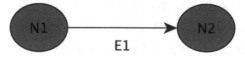

Figure 2-1. *Simple graph*

© Louis Davidson 2023
L. Davidson, *Practical Graph Structures in SQL Server and Azure SQL*,
https://doi.org/10.1007/978-1-4842-9459-8_2

You need a table to hold the N1 and N2 nodes. These nodes could be of the same type or different types. For example, they could be one person being the friend or family member of the other, or a person being a fan of a certain football team. Let's assume for this example that they are the same type (and in the future, if I want them to be two different types of objects, I will label the nodes as such).

For my examples, I will use data that would be at home in many relational tables for most examples, simply because that is how you will typically think of the data. In the following two chapters, I will establish how SQL Server implements graph structures, but for now, just take the data structures to be basically as you have built in SQL Server tables before. To implement the structure in Figure 2-1, say you have the following rows in a table to represent the two nodes:

```
Node
------
N1
N2
```

Now you need a data structure that represents the edge, like this:

```
FromNode   ToNode
--------   -------
N1         N2
```

A common term for this data structure is an **adjacency list**. The goal is to store a list of nodes adjacent to each other in the graph. Except for one very specialized (and quite common) graph data structure (a tree, which I will define later in the chapter), this is the way to implement a graph in a database. Even Microsoft SQL Server's graph objects are implemented this way **internally**. It is common to use the term **neighbor** or **parent/child** to describe the relationship between nodes. Parent and child are very common for acyclic relationships, and neighbor is for cases where you are recording that two nodes are next to one another and the relationship allows cycles. The child/neighbor node in a relationship is the one that is represented in the ToNode column.

In practice, beyond the key values, you will always have additional columns in your node tables, and usually in your edge tables as well. Using the edge data structures' from and to columns, plus other columns, you can create many different shapes of graphs by applying one or more unique indexes on different columns, as well as using other methods to limit the types of data that can be placed in a column. This is what I will introduce in the rest of this chapter.

I will discuss two major types of graph configurations, **acyclic** and **cyclic**. From Chapter 1, it is hopefully clear that the primary differentiator between them is that one allows cycles in the edges and the other doesn't. Of course, the other differentiator is the type of situations where these data structures are useful.

An acyclic graph is often useful to define something very structured, whereas a cyclic graph is useful for more organic scenarios. This will become clearer in each of the major sections.

Acyclic Graphs

The easiest graphs to work with in a relational database are acyclic. The reason comes down to the method used to process graphs in a relational setting, the **breadth-first algorithm** (or **relational recursion**). This algorithm was created for relational processing, because the typical recursion used to process these data structures did not fit well with the set-based nature of a relational database.

For example, consider the graph in Figure 2-2.

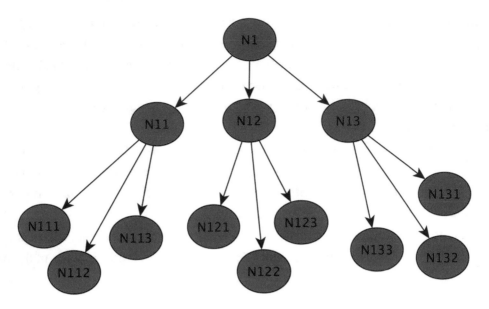

Figure 2-2. *Sample graph structure*

Processing this using a typical recursive manner, you choose your starting point as N1 and then see if this node has one unprocessed child. It does, so fetch N11. See if N11 has unprocessed children. Yes, N111. N111 has no unprocessed child nodes, so whatever you are doing with the data of the node, you add that to an output data structure. Then step back up to N11 and get the next child node. And keep going. This is referred to as a **depth-first algorithm**.

Common operations are counting nodes, summing sales from that node, and so on. For your example, let's just say you are counting child nodes. So, you recurse back to N11 and add 1 to the child count. Then you check for more child nodes, and you have more. Over and over. You stop when every node has been processed in the subgraph that started with your starting point.

This works great for certain kinds of programming languages but terrible for relational ones where set-based processing is the clearly desired method of programming. It works with sets of data, so that is the kind of processing that has been devised for working with graphs in the manner that relations engines work.

For a breadth-first algorithm, instead of digging down in the structure, you take a starting point and then get all of the children of that node. Then the children of those nodes, all at once. Taking that same diagram, let's break this down into a series of three queries on the data, as seen in Figure 2-3.

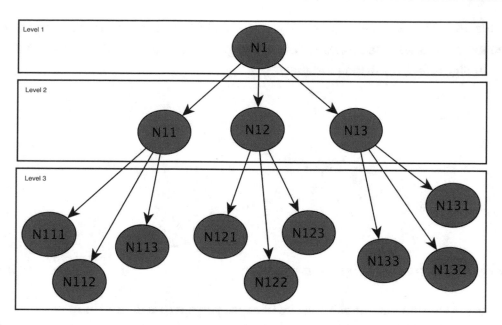

Figure 2-3. *Sample graph indicating the different levels that will be fetched in a breadth-first query*

You query for the starting point. In this case, it's one node, but it could be any number of nodes (in fact, that is the basis of some of the code in this book to do things like starting at every node simultaneously!). Your breadth-first algorithm is to query:

```
SELECT GraphId
FROM   GraphObject
WHERE GraphId = @startingPoint --starting point = N1
```

The next step is to take that set of data and query:

```
SELECT GraphId
FROM   GraphObject
WHERE GraphId in (GraphId values from previous query)
```

From the diagram, this gives you a set with N11, N12, N13. The next query does the same join, but the GraphId from the previous query is now these three nodes. You can sum/count/etc. during each loop through the data. There is more to it, clearly, which will become clearer when I implement the non-pseudo-code, but this is the gist of the algorithm.

This process is pretty easy for an acyclic graph, but you can probably already start to see the difficulties when working with cyclic graph structures, in that if you have the graph in Figure 2-4, it will loop eternally.

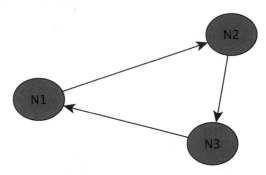

Figure 2-4. *Sample graph with a cycle*

Many operations stop making sense because you have an eternal loop when processing this with a naïve nested loop algorithm.

One thing to note: If you have been taught repeatedly that relational processes should avoid iterative code, this may shock you a little. Practically all graph processing is iterative. Any code you write, and any code that Microsoft uses to implement its graph structures, is iterative. The trick will be to make sure the amount you iterate is the least possible and is as efficient as possible. There are some alternative methods of processing when dealing with tree algorithms, one of which will be covered in Chapter 6.

Trees

By far the most common graph that has been implemented in relational databases for many years is a **tree**. A tree is a structure that requires that every node have either zero or one parent, and no more. Consider a real tree (or in the case of Figure 2-5, a glorious reproduction of a tree from Disney's Animal Kingdom theme park).

Figure 2-5. *A not-exactly-live tree as an analogy for a tree structure*

It has one trunk that goes into the ground. Either direction out (down to the roots or up to the branches), you can see the analogy. Any branch can be from the trunk or another branch, but it can only be one of these. Branches don't grow together and reform as one. (At least not typically, and this isn't botany class!) Nodes that do not have any child nodes are referred to as leaf nodes, much like the leaves on the branches stand alone.

My breadth-first example structure was a tree, reincluded as Figure 2-6.

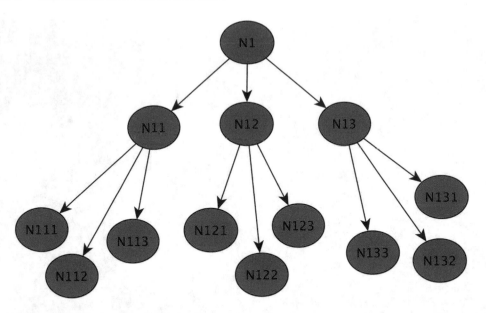

Figure 2-6. *Example tree repeated*

To represent this in an adjacency list structure, you have rows like

```
From      To
____-     ____-
N1        N11
N11       N111
N11       N112
N11       N113
N1        N12
```

And so on. In order to make sure that the tree is always a tree, you need to protect one main condition: unique **to** values. Since a child row can only have one parent in a tree, having a uniqueness constraint on that column of the adjacency list ensures it is a tree.

The other thing you typically need to do is include a constraint of some sort to make sure that the from value does not equal the to value. This is the only cycle that the uniqueness constraint will not stop (though a duplicated to and from value basically makes the row a root and a leaf and would likely be discovered quickly...but one of my mottos is that *bad data doesn't happen if you don't let it occur at all*).

While all tree structures require a single root, a table structure such as this could contain multiple tree structures. In some cases, a row with NULL, N1 could be included in the structure as the starting point when you create the tree. You can make sure there is only one using a unique index, which only allows one NULL value. (SQL Server treats a NULL value as distinct in indexes, unlike in comparisons, so that would make sure that you had only one root node.). You could allow greater than one root node by using a filtered UNIQUE index that ignores NULL values. If you want to make sure the NULL row is never deleted, a trigger object can be used, which is especially useful if you have users that can delete rows in an ad-hoc manner.

If you need to model multiple tree structures, it is possible to just create multiple edge objects, each with a distinct purpose. For example, consider a company reporting structure. There are multiple projects going on where a person is in the project management hierarchy, and typically there is a hierarchy for dealing with HR type things. So, you could create

```
ManagementEdge (FromEmployee, ToEmployee)
```

And you could also create the same table again for every project.

```
Project1 (FromEmployee, ToEmployee)
Project2 (FromEmployee, ToEmployee)
```

Alternatively, you could model this as one structure that allows for many trees to coincide in the same structure.

```
ReportingHierarchy (FromEmployee, ToEmployee, HierarchyName)
```

All the indexes discussed for the general tree structures would still make sense, but you would include the HierarchyName in the object because the uniqueness stands only for one project if an employee can be on multiple projects.

It might just make sense to have the ManagementEdge as modeled, but then have the project hierarchy be in its own ProjectManagementEdge since they serve different purposes. Determining how to model your graph is pretty much the same challenge as with any database: making the structures match your requirements with the tightness to prevent bad data and the flexibility to do what the customer wants to do.

Finally, note that you can implement variations of parent cardinalities to implement strict types of trees. For example, a **binary** or **simple tree** is defined as a tree where you can only have two children for each node. Consider Figure 2-7.

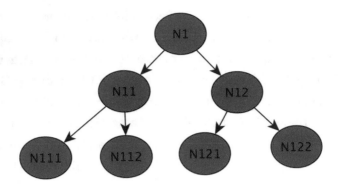

Figure 2-7. *Sample binary tree*

One consideration you must have for creating a binary tree (or really any limited cardinality of child row) is how to make sure a node that violates the structure child is not created. There are a few methods that work. Using triggers to count the number of nodes is one, as is adding a node number and using a check constraint to only allow values of 1 and 2, along with a unique index on the from item.

So

```
BinaryTree (FromNode, ToNode, NodeNumber (Values IN 1, 2), UNIQUE (From,
NodeNumber);
```

The downside is that you have this column that seems to indicate an order to the nodes that is important. (In some systems you may desire that ordering, perhaps to guide the user in a direction or to sort the nodes.)

It can also be argued that some data integrity of this sort could be deferred, and you simply check after changes have been made and fix issues later, especially if your requirements get more complicated. Regardless of *how* you make sure integrity is enforced, it needs to be enforced.

Another important concept when working with trees is how **balanced** the tree is. For example, consider Figure 2-8.

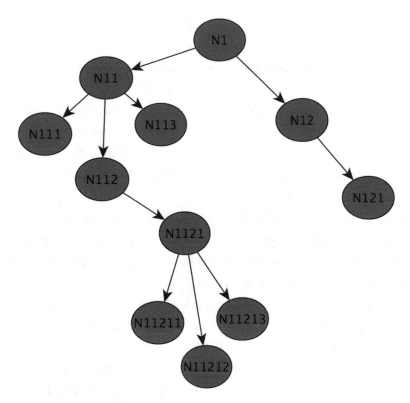

Figure 2-8. *An unbalanced tree*

When using a breadth-first algorithm, a very balanced, **shallow** (that is, less hops from root to leaf nodes) structure is quicker to process since you will have less iterations to go through. This can be very important if you are making a tree to search with an index to some data or just a fact of life if you are representing something in the real world that is what it is.

Note   In Chapter 6, I will introduce and demonstrate an alternative method of implementing tree structures made possible by the rigid nature of their structures.

Other Acyclic Graphs

While trees are straightforward enough to implement using a basic adjacency list format (including making sure that the data actually fits the strict requirements of only one parent and no cycles), other acyclic graph types are not quite so simple because they are more flexible in structure.

Common acyclic graph examples that we all generally encounter are bills of materials, geographies, and classifications. Geographies are useful in many ways. For example, you could model the world as the root, then continent, region, and so on. Or perhaps country, then state, province, and down to city or postal code.

One of the more universal examples of an acyclic graph that isn't a tree is that of a bill of materials. This data structure is a very simple, straightforward example that we should all be able to visualize. A bill of materials is a breakdown of all the pieces and parts that make up some product. In Chapter 7, I will implement a bill of materials that contains the parts of a fictional shelf product.

For example, when you buy a car, it is a single item you purchase. But that car has many parts that make up that single unit of purchase. For simplicity, let's just start with the engine. The engine is a menagerie of parts that contains other parts. And those parts are often made up of other parts, generally right down to screws, washers, bolts, and nuts. Many of the parts that make up that car are also sold individually as well.

The car's breakdown is, in and of itself, be a tree. But many of the parts and assemblies can be in more than one vehicle type.

For a very simple example, consider a company that makes frames. They have an 11-inch frame and a 10-inch frame, and they both use the same hanging kit. See Figure 2-9.

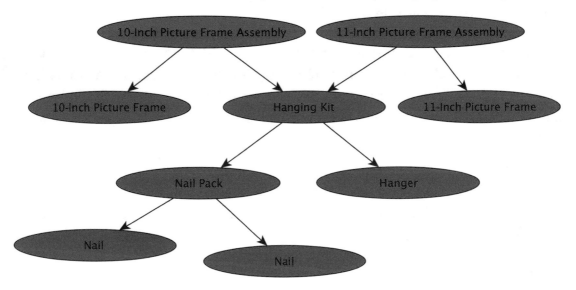

Figure 2-9. *Simple bill of materials*

While items can have more than one predecessor in the graph (in Figure 2-9, you can see that the Hanging Kit has two predecessors), every starting node you pick can be treated as if it was the root node of a tree. Start at the Hanging Kit, and you get a tree where the next level nodes are Hanger and Nail Pack. The Nail Pack contains two Nails (in your actual implementation, you will use a magnitude on the Nail Pack to Nail edge to represent multiples. I will discuss more about edge magnitudes in Chapter 3 because this is important to some designs).

Hence, when you traverse/process a bill of materials (or any acyclic graph), you often can treat it like a tree when fetching the child rows, not having to worry about cycles. When you load the bill of materials structure, this is when you must make sure to not introduce a cycle. Unlike trees where you can limit a node to exist in only one parent row with an index, in this case you cannot protect against cycles with a simple constraint.

Note that, depending on the tools you are using, the idea of treating parts of a bill of materials like a tree may fall apart if you need to see the entire structure due to how some graph code works. This will be clearer in Chapters 3 and 7.

As you are adding nodes to a polyhierarchy, you need to do a query to search for cycles. Like the example back in Figure 2-4 (repeated as Figure 2-10), consider this graph before the edge between N3 and N1 was added.

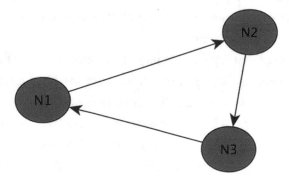

Figure 2-10. *Graph with a cycle*

All would have been fine. But that new edge from N3 to N1 creates a cycle. Finding the cycle condition will basically use the breadth-first algorithm discussed previously, but in this case, your query is looking for a match to the node where you start. So, for each iteration, you are looking for FirstNodeId = CurrentNodeId; if found, then this is no longer an acyclic graph (and you will have to take the appropriate action, like rolling back the insert of that edge).

This can be done in a stored procedure or even a trigger if you want to keep the cycle from happening at all. Of course, if you need optimum performance, you might have to defer cycle checking (especially for very large graphs), although this also has downsides if the data is also actively queried.

As I go through the examples in the book, I will frequently use a stored procedure to manage and query new nodes because rarely are the user key values the internal values you use for surrogate keys. Hence, the user need only know that Fred and Bob are friends, not any internal details. It is also very useful because some of the code you write may need to be tuned as you start to get to very large graphs.

Cyclic Graphs

Cyclic graphs, as the name implies, allow cycles to show up in the graph. The allowance of cycles generally means that you won't do as much math with the nodes, like summing sales of subordinate nodes; rather, it will be more likely be exploring the relationships between nodes.

There are a few memorable uses of graphs that you use every day such as on websites where you order products. They capture your buying history in a graph structure and use your similarity to other users to see if they can make you even more like them by telling you what others like you have also ordered.

The most famous graph that you probably have heard of is the basis of the movie/play *Six Degrees of Separation*. The theory is that everyone is no more than six friend connections from anyone else on earth. The most famous of this is with Kevin Bacon.

One thing you will start noticing about many of the designs housed in your relational databases is that a lot of the relationships you find can be modeled as a node-to-node relationships. For example, think of a typical sales order system as shown in the conceptual model in Figure 2-11.

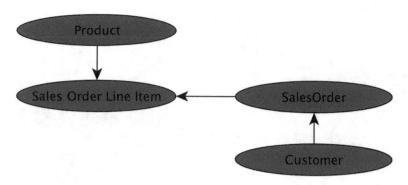

Figure 2-11. *Conceptual model of a sales system*

When you are analyzing customer's interest, knowing what products they have ordered, returned, looked at, and such is very useful. You can take this product order relationship and put it into a couple of nodes, as shown in Figure 2-12.

Figure 2-12. *Segment of a graph relating product to customer*

You can put the relationship either from customer to product or product to customer (or both, as we will discuss). Software can generally traverse the relationship in both directions, though typically not simultaneously. (We will discuss that concept in the non-directed graph section). The trick is to always carefully name the edge in a way that indicates what the relationship is, such as `Product-Purchased->Customer` or `Customer-Ordered (or Was Interested In)->Product`.

I mentioned that when implementing a directed graph, you simply need to look for the newly inserted (or updated) node in the same path and you were sure there were no cycles. Consider the graph in Figure 2-13, which has multiple cycles.

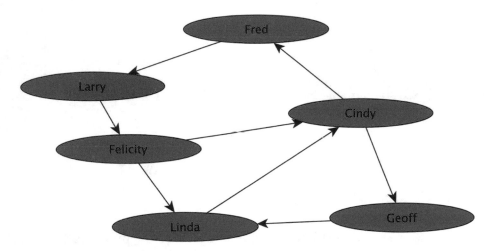

Figure 2-13. *Sample graph with cycles*

When writing the code to process this graph to find connections to Fred, you will see that every node is connected, and there are several cycles in the graph, two that lead back to Fred, as shown in Figures 2-14 and 2-15.

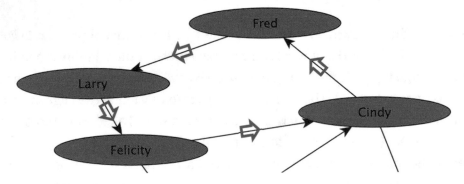

Figure 2-14. *Cycle from Fred -> Larry -> Felicity -> Cindy -> Fred*

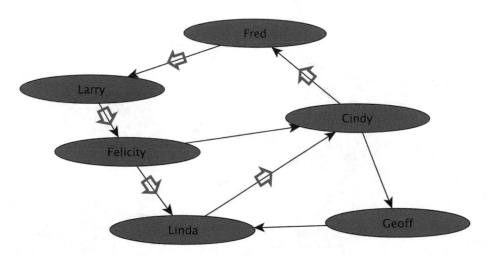

Figure 2-15. *Cycle from Fred -> Larry -> Felicity -> Linda -> Cindy -> Fred*

Each of these cycles back to Fred, so you have an obvious stopping point.

You have also now touched the Cindy node twice. This isn't necessarily a cycle because you have hit the same node twice. However, it does mean that you will begin repeating results because the subsequent tree traversal is always the same after repeated nodes. Generally, you want to terminate one of the processing paths because it will yield repeated results and wasted processing time.

Note   I won't delve into it in this chapter, but in a diagram like this, the edges could be defined differently. Fred -> Larry could be Likes, and Larry -> Felicity could be Dislikes. Whether this is a cycle or not can be up to how you need to traverse the structure.

But in Figure 2-16, this cycle is more of a challenge.

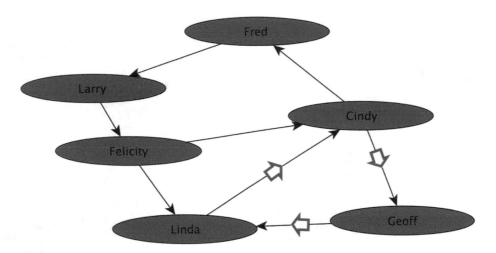

Figure 2-16. *Cycle from Cindy -> Geoff -> Linda -> Cindy, not back to the*
starting node

Now not only do you need to make sure to stop processing when you cycle back to
the starting node, but also anywhere in the graph. (Note that this was not an issue when
you were looking for cycles in the directed graph because you were only dealing with
adding an edge.) If you start to add many edges at a time, you may also need to be aware
of these kinds of eternal loops that could arise in processing.

This all leads to the most common operation with a network like this, that of finding
a **shortest path** from any two nodes, which is Fred to Geoff in the last example. There are
two paths to get from Fred to Geoff:

- Fred -> Larry -> Felicity -> Cindy -> Geoff

- Fred -> Larry -> Felicity -> Linda -> Cindy -> Geoff

The first is clearly the path between the two nodes that is shortest, with a length of 4.
You may also want to see the longest path (the scenic route) in some cases.

In some cases, you may want to have **weighted nodes**. For example, consider the
case when you are building a map type solution. Say you have the graph in Figure 2-17,
which implements a kind of map from an entrance node to a destination node.

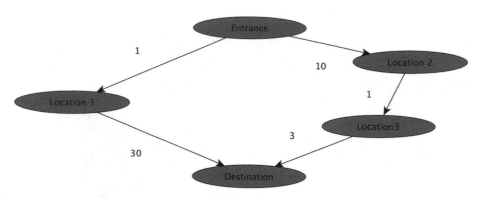

Figure 2-17. *Graph with weighted edges*

When you have weighted edges, like distances, the shortest path based on hops may not always be the shortest or cheapest path to traverse the graph. You can't start eliminating non-crossing paths either, because as you see in this example, Entrance to Location 1 is 1 unit, but it is 10 to get to Location 2. But the next hop from Location 1 is 30 units, whereas from Location 2 to Destination through 3, this is only 4. So, the shortest weighted path is the longer path in hops.

Non-Directed Graphs

Directed graphs have edges that only state a relationship one way. Fred -> Follows -> Bob. It does say that Fred follows Bob, but it doesn't say that Bob follows Fred. In a non-directed graph, every edge states a relationship that goes both ways.

While you can only really implement a directed graph, sometimes you want to implement something that behaves like each edge is not directed, and that if Fred is connected to Bob, Bob is connected to Fred too. In this case, you need to make sure that there are two directed edges between every related node. This, of course, introduces far more cycles than in a normal graph for a few reasons. Consider the graph from Figure 2-18.

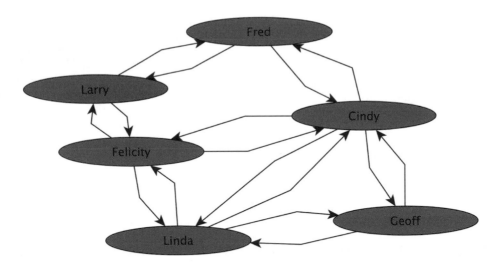

Figure 2-18. *Graph from Figure 2-13 with simulated non-directed edges*

In the directed form, you had three major cycles. In this graph, every relationship between nodes is a cycle. And then every path becomes more cycles.

This may seem like something you wouldn't want to do, but this is similar to how the six degrees of separation example would be manifested. This is because the primary graph you will work with is Person -> Worked With -> Person (or perhaps more specifically Person -> Performed On -> Work <- Performed On <- Person). If John Wayne worked with Lucille Ball on *I Love Lucy*, the latter would also be true that Lucile Ball worked with John Wayne. (Or, as noted, it will be implemented as something like Lucile Ball worked on *I Love Lucy* episode "Lucy and Harpo Marx" and Harpo Marx worked on that episode too.)

It is important to realize this when you are designing your graph solutions to note if the relationships you are implementing should really indicate a reciprocal relationship (and make sure your software inserts, deletes, and updates both edge rows as a group).

Summary

In this chapter, you got a high-level look at the different algorithms you will be building example code for in this book. You started out by exploring the algorithm that will define a large amount of the code in this book, either internally using specialized graph database syntax or in code you need to write to do specialized operations. (This will be clearer in the next chapter when I discuss how to use the graph objects.)

You then learned the definitions of different types of graphs and the basics of how you will use them to model different scenarios and then implement them. Acyclic graphs are for things like trees to define rigid structures like file systems, jurisdictions, and genealogies. Another example is a bill of materials, where a row might have multiple predecessors in the structure but a cycle in the structure wouldn't make sense (since a bill of materials defines the parts that make up other parts and products, and a cycle would defy the laws of physics).

Cyclic graph implementations in a relational database aren't really new (most many-to-many relationship are actually cyclic graphs in disguise) but they process them as graphs and using multiple many-to-many relationships simultaneously (which you will see in the next chapter).

Finally, you looked at several optimizations that you can use to improve the processing speed of tree structures. This can be helpful because trees are frequently involved in reporting or checking hierarchies for security, as examples.

CHAPTER 3

SQL Graph Table Basics

In this chapter (and the next), it is time to start coding graph node and edge tables in Transact-SQL code. I will walk you through all the graph syntax and techniques you will need for the rest of the book and to build your own graph solutions.

The syntax of the graph extensions to SQL Server, and even the internals of how the graph objects are created, is probably going to be weird to you. It was (and still kind of is) to me. Some of it is based on standard graph syntax that you may have encountered if you are not new to graph database code outside of SQL Server. I will approach the code in this book like SQL Server's engine is the only engine you have and need for graph implementation on a computer. This is not really the case, and if you are trying to implement a database that is essentially only a graph, you should read about pure graph databases and consider them as an alternative.

My expectation for this book is that you generally know the T-SQL language, know the basics of relational databases, and want to extend your relational databases with elements of a graph database.

Note If you want to know more about designing relational databases, check out my book *Pro SQL Server Relational Database Design and Implementation*, also published by Apress.

Later in the book, I will provide additional tools to implement graphs and tree structures (a single parent only DAG (directed acyclic graph), abbreviated because the word acyclic is hard to spell!), but this two-chapter introduction to the SQL Server graph syntax will serve as a jumping off point for the rest of the book.

In this chapter, you will implement a simple set of graph objects, load them, and see how to code them. The next chapter will go into some techniques to make loading and tuning your objects easier. The code for this and all chapters can be downloaded at https://github.com/Apress/practical-graph-structures.

© Louis Davidson 2023
L. Davidson, *Practical Graph Structures in SQL Server and Azure SQL*,
https://doi.org/10.1007/978-1-4842-9459-8_3

Object Creation

In the downloads, you start with a database created with no parameters (so it will be basically as it is in your model database). Nothing you will do in this database will require any performance tuning at all.

```
CREATE DATABASE TestGraph
GO
USE TestGraph
GO
```

The graph you are going to start with has the shape shown in Figure 3-1. Each of the nodes represents a "follow" relationship that you will implement. Later you will add several other types of nodes and edges to the graph via the examples. (The naming of the "people" in the graph is done to make the names memorable and in no way references any people in the world.)

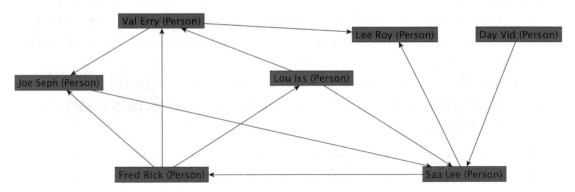

Figure 3-1. *Graph with Person nodes connected by Follows edges*

Creating your node and edge objects in SQL Server is exactly like creating any other table. The syntax is basically the same with only one thing different. You need to tell each object that it is a node or an edge. In the following script, you will create the objects needed to implement this graph.

First, you create a schema, as you typically never want to put any objects in the dbo schema. Using a specific schema for your objects is great for segmenting objects and never accidentally creating a bunch of objects in your master database.

```
IF SCHEMA_ID('Network') IS NULL
    EXEC ('CREATE SCHEMA Network');
```

For the person table, you give a person `FirstName` and `LastName` attributes, as well as a computed column to hold a concatenation of the two names. I often use the `Name` attribute in examples, but I did want to show some cases where you need to get multiple attributes in the Transact-SQL code. These first two objects also have a `Value` column that I will use for demonstrating mathematical aggregates.

```
CREATE TABLE Network.Person
(
    PersonId  int IDENTITY CONSTRAINT PKPerson PRIMARY KEY,
    FirstName nvarchar(100) NULL,
    LastName  nvarchar(100) NOT NULL,
    Name      AS (CONCAT(FirstName + ' ', LastName))PERSISTED,
    Value     int NOT NULL
                        CONSTRAINT DFLTPerson_Value DEFAULT(1),
    CONSTRAINT AKPerson UNIQUE(FirstName,LastName)
) AS NODE;
```

Just by adding the AS NODE to the typical table declaration, this is now a NODE object. In a few pages you will explore what that actually means internally. Next, create the EDGE object that you will start with:

```
CREATE TABLE Network.Follows
(Value INT NOT NULL
      CONSTRAINT DFLTFollows_Value DEFAULT(1)
) AS EDGE;
```

Note that you don't need any columns at all, so this would also be an acceptable table declaration:

```
CREATE TABLE Network.Follows
AS EDGE;
```

You can list the NODE and EDGE objects in the `sys.tables` system view:

```
SELECT OBJECT_SCHEMA_NAME(tables.object_id) AS schema_name,
       tables.name AS table_name,
       tables.is_edge,
       tables.is_node
```

```
FROM    sys.tables
WHERE   tables.is_edge = 1
   OR tables.is_node = 1;
```

After executing these scripts (which are also available at the book's official GitHub repository at https://github.com/Apress/practical-graph-structures), the output of this statement is

```
schema_name          table_name          is_edge is_node
----------------     ---------------     ------- -------

Network              Person                 0       1
Network              Follows                1       0
```

At this point you have the objects ready for the next step of adding some data. Note that the examples in the book are done in T-SQL code only but you can find the objects in Management Studio in the Object Explorer, as you can see in Figure 3-2.

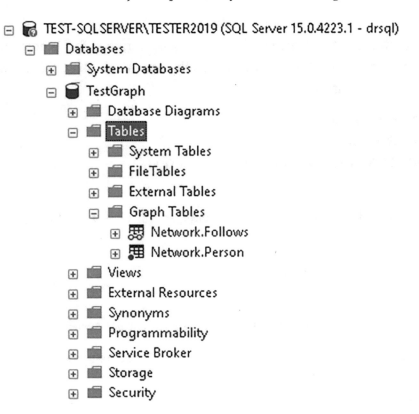

Figure 3-2. *Management Studio location of Graph Tables folder*

If you are using Azure Data studio, the graph tables show up in the list like relational tables.

Creating Data

When you get to adding rows to your tables, adding rows to a NODE object is exactly like adding rows to any table. You can use any of the syntaxes you use to create data in basic relational tables. All of the internal graph columns will be automatically managed (unless you directly manage their values, which will be covered in Chapter 4).

Let's create some data in the Network.Person object:

```
INSERT INTO Network.Person(FirstName, LastName)
VALUES('Fred', 'Rick'),
      ('Lou', 'Iss'),
      ('Val', 'Erry'),
      ('Lee', 'Roy'),
      ('Saa', 'Lee'),
      ('Joe', 'Seph'),
      ('Day', 'Vid');
```

Next, let's look at some data from the table using SELECT * to get all the columns:

```
SELECT *
FROM    Network.Person
WHERE   Person.FirstName = 'Fred'
   AND Person.LastName = 'Rick';
```

The results are interesting. You not only see some extra columns, but they also have really hard-to-work-with names. The first outputted column looks something like this:

```
$node_id_C580185613BB42EF81F4A68F6FA539DC
---------------------------------------------------------------
{"type":"node","schema":"Network","table":"Person","id":0}
```

The value is an encoding of a few internal columns (which I will cover later), but you can see from the JSON view that this is a node, the schema and table names, and then an internal id value. That internal id is part of the graph database engine. It is not the same as the identity column in your table, but it is very similar. (Although, as you will see later, it is a lot easier to insert your own values into!)

The rest of the table is what you expect to be:

PersonId	FirstName	LastName	Name	Value
1	Fred	Rick	Fred Rick	1

You can use the complex column name in a query (surrounded by square brackets, because $ as the lead character tells SQL Server that a column name is a pseudocolumn):

```
SELECT [$node_id_C580185613BB42EF81F4A68F6FA539DC]
FROM    Network.Person
WHERE [$node_id_C580185613BB42EF81F4A68F6FA539DC]   =
'{"type":"node","schema":"Network","table":"Person","id":0}';
```

This code returns the same JSON as before. Leave off the square brackets and you get the following error:

```
Msg 126, Level 15, State 2, Line 69
Invalid pseudocolumn "$node_id_3949CAAFE93D496C9A4CF1F33767B666".
```

A **pseudocolumn** is a SQL Server construct that lets you use a value without knowing its exact name. There are others, particularly in partitioning. Here, you use $node_id instead of this value (which will change when you create this table on your machine in all probability):

```
--not in square brackets, because this is not a column name
SELECT Person.$node_id
FROM    Network.Person
WHERE  Person.$node_id = '{"type":"node","schema":"Network","table":"Person
","id":0}';
```

For the edge you created, there are several more complex column names that you will use pseudocolumns to work with, as you can see after executing the following code:

```
SELECT *
FROM    Network.Follows;
```

This returns the following output (you haven't loaded any data yet, so you are just looking at the structure):

```
$edge_id_3E64B3D47C09432595C25D1FB2146A35
-------------------------------------------


$from_id_AA09B7FBEA714F918B3C0D19A8B24A0A
-------------------------------------------


$to_id_4E49D534C24E4F4D8E0E0D207237A425
-------------------------------------------
```

There is also a Value column added on the edge for later usage.

These are all abbreviated as $edge_id, $from_id, $to_id. The latter two take as input a $node_id from a node to identify the from and to nodes in the relationship. When doing the input of data, the basic pattern is something like the following (in the next chapter, I will show some other data creation patterns). The basic format is that you need to look up the $from_id and the $to_id values in a subquery:

```
INSERT INTO Network.Follows($from_id, $to_id)
SELECT (    SELECT Person.$node_id
            FROM    Network.Person
            WHERE   Person.FirstName = 'Fred'
                AND Person.LastName = 'Rick') AS from_id,
       (    SELECT Person.$node_id
            FROM    Network.Person
            WHERE   Person.FirstName = 'Joe'
                AND Person.LastName = 'Seph') AS to_id;
--from_id and to_id just names to make it easier to see when
--debugging. It can be whatever.
```

Looking at that data now, you can see

```
SELECT *
FROM    Network.Follows;
```

The output has four columns. Note that your column names will almost certainly differ, and you may have different id values too.

```
$edge_id_3E64B3D47C09432595C25D1FB2146A35
-----------------------------------------------------------
{"type":"edge","schema":"Network","table":"Follows","id":0}

 $from_id_AA09B7FBEA714F918B3C0D19A8B24A0A
 -----------------------------------------------------------
 {"type":"node","schema":"Network","table":"Person","id":0}

$to_id_4E49D534C24E4F4D8E0E0D207237A425
-----------------------------------------------------------
{"type":"node","schema":"Network","table":"Person","id":5}
```

You can also do this using the textual values just like any other table. (First, clear the table, as you have not protected against duplication yet, which I will show in the next chapter.)

```
TRUNCATE TABLE Network.Follows;

--using truncate so the id values are reset, just for clarity
--in my examples. No need to do this in real use, and in this
--case it doesn't matter that much.
```

Now you can just insert the row again using the textual values:

```
INSERT INTO Network.Follows($from_id, $to_id) VALUES
('{"type":"node","schema":"Network","table":"Person","id":0}',
'{"type":"node","schema":"Network","table":"Person","id":5}');
```

Note that these items are values you can directly enter, but they are not the actual values that are stored in the SQL Server. Internally there are a couple of bigint columns that are represented. (In the next chapter, I will show you more about how data is formatted internally and how you can use this textual format to your advantage when loading data from an outside source.)

In the downloads, the rest of the rows will be inserted using the first lookup-based format, with the SELECT statements separated by UNION ALL operators. Next, let's show the data that has been created.

The following query is something you rarely want to do, as the goal will be to rarely if ever get internal values directly. In the next few pages, I will start to introduce how to query this data using the SQL graph operators. However, this query is directly analogous to what our simplest graph query will do, and it is useful to know how to do this because there is nothing like an OUTER JOIN using the SQL graph operators.

```
SELECT Person.Name AS PersonName,
       FollowedPerson.Name AS FollowedPersonName
FROM   Network.Person
       JOIN Network.Follows
           ON Person.$node_id = Follows.$from_id
       JOIN Network.Person AS FollowedPerson
           ON FollowedPerson.$node_id = Follows.$to_id;
```

The output of this query is every edge you created, displaying the name of the person and the name of the person they follow:

PersonName	FollowedPersonName
Fred Rick	Joe Seph
Fred Rick	Lou Iss
Joe Seph	Saa Lee
Saa Lee	Lee Roy
Val Erry	Joe Seph
Val Erry	Lee Roy
Lou Iss	Saa Lee
Lou Iss	Val Erry
Saa Lee	Fred Rick
Fred Rick	Val Erry
Day Vid	Saa Lee

If you go back to Figure 3-1, you can trace every line from the end with no arrow to the end with an arrow in that list.

Querying Data

Querying data using the SQL Graph operators is a bit complex, but the code it replaces is also complex. In the previous section, you queried the data using `JOIN` operators, but in the next sections that code will be expressed in a much more compact manner. This compactness comes with a modicum of complexity.

You will look at two levels of querying data. First, you will look at straightforward node-to-node queries where you know how far along the path you want to look for a match. Second, you will look at traversing all the possible paths, looking for a way to connect nodes that are a variable length apart.

Node-to-Node Querying

The first task to learn when coding with SQL graph objects is how the queries work. They are very different at times from the normal SQL queries you probably have written. The big difference is that you will be querying the graph engine that has been written to work with just the one type of data. It is complex data, but since it is one specific special pattern, the syntax is a lot more general.

The syntax you will use is a `MATCH` expression. It returns a Boolean TRUE or FALSE for what is basically internally a join or set of joins. As an example, the following is the query from a few pages ago rewritten using the `MATCH` expression:

```
SELECT      Person.Name AS PersonName,
            FollowedPerson.Name AS FollowedPersonName
FROM        Network.Person,
            Network.Follows,
            Network.Person AS FollowedPerson
WHERE MATCH(Person-(Follows)->FollowedPerson);
```

The output of this query is as from the previous query (perhaps sorted differently since there is no `ORDER BY` clause). Let me break this down.

```
FROM        Network.Person,
            Network.Follows,
            Network.Person AS FollowedPerson
```

One of the weirdest quirks with the graph query syntax is that you cannot use any ANSI-92 style joins in the query when you are using a MATCH expression, not even the equivalent CROSS JOIN for the commas. Attempt this following query:

```
SELECT      CAST(Person.Name AS nvarchar(20)) AS PersonName,
            FollowedPerson.Name AS FollowedPersonName
FROM        Network.Person
            CROSS JOIN Network.Follows
            CROSS JOIN Network.Person AS FollowedPerson
WHERE MATCH(Person-(Follows)->FollowedPerson);
```

You will be greeting with the following error:

```
Msg 13920, Level 16, State 1, Line 221
Identifier 'Follows' in a MATCH clause is used with a JOIN clause or APPLY
operator. JOIN and APPLY are not supported with MATCH clauses.
```

You will also see two more error messages for Person and FollowedPerson. Any additional joins to fetch additional data will need to be acquired in a different manner (example to follow).

```
FROM        Network.Person,
            Network.Follows,
            Network.Person AS FollowedPerson
WHERE MATCH(Person-(Follows)->FollowedPerson);
```

Now take the MATCH clause. Using a kind of ASCII art, the most basic MATCH clause has ObjectName-(Edge)->OtherObjectName and loosely translates to joining ObjectName to Edge and Edge to OtherObjectName. If your only use of SQL Graph is to implement a single many-to-many relationship, it may not be worth it to use these objects. However, as I will show in this chapter and the rest of the book, you can write some very complex connections through multiple edges and nodes to ask complex questions in a manner that is actually easier to understand (once you understand the fairly complex nature of the MATCH expression).

As noted, you cannot do any ANSI style joins in your graph table query, so you have two choices. You can either use a CTE to fetch the graph results and then join your additional results, like the following:

```
WITH GraphPart AS (
SELECT      Person.Name AS PersonName,
            FollowedPerson.Name AS FollowedPersonName,
            Person.FirstName
FROM        Network.Person,
            Network.Follows,
            Network.Person AS FollowedPerson
WHERE MATCH(Person-(Follows)->FollowedPerson))

SELECT GraphPart.PersonName, GraphPart.FollowedPersonName,
        Colors.ColorName
FROM    GraphPart
        --This could also be a CTE or a real table
        JOIN (SELECT 'blue' AS ColorName
               UNION ALL
              SELECT 'red') AS Colors
            ON CASE WHEN GraphPart.FirstName = 'Fred'
                         THEN 'blue'
                      ELSE 'red'
                  END = Colors.ColorName;
```

Or you can just separate your other tables, views, or (as I have used) derived tables in the comma-delimited list in the FROM clause:

```
SELECT      CAST(Person.Name AS nvarchar(20)) AS PersonName,
            FollowedPerson.Name AS FollowedPersonName,
            Colors.ColorName
FROM        Network.Person,
            Network.Follows,
            Network.Person AS FollowedPerson,
            (   SELECT 'blue' AS ColorName
                UNION ALL
                SELECT 'red') AS Colors
WHERE MATCH(Person-(Follows)->FollowedPerson)
                --join clause to the derived table
                AND CASE WHEN Person.FirstName = 'Fred'
```

```
        THEN 'blue'
    ELSE 'red'
END = Colors.ColorName;
```

Because of not being able to do ANSI-92 join syntax, there is no way to do an OUTER JOIN, so you need to take care to write your joins safely to not lose data accidentally that you wanted to return.

Filtering Output

When you want to filter the output of a query using the base MATCH expression, you filter the output the same as in any query. So, to just see the people that Lou Iss follows,

```
SELECT Person.Name AS PersonName,
       FollowedPerson.Name AS FollowedPersonName
FROM   Network.Person,
       Network.Follows,
       Network.Person AS FollowedPerson
WHERE  Person.FirstName = 'Lou'
   AND Person.LastName = 'Iss'
   AND MATCH(Person-(Follows)->FollowedPerson);
```

This returns just people with a PersonName of Lou Iss. In Figure 3-3, you can see the paths that are traversed.

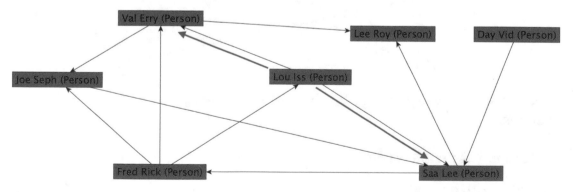

Figure 3-3. *Paths followed in a MATCH clause from Lou Iss to directly related Persons*

The results from the query are

```
PersonName            FollowedPersonName
------------------    --------------------
Lou Iss               Saa Lee
Lou Iss               Val Erry
```

The first query gave you people that a person follows. To find people that follow a person, reverse the arrow in the MATCH operator:

```
SELECT FollowedPerson.Name AS Person, Person.Name AS Follows
FROM   Network.Person,
       Network.Follows,
       Network.Person AS FollowedPerson
WHERE  Person.FirstName = 'Lou'
   AND Person.LastName = 'Iss'
   AND MATCH(Person<-(Follows)-FollowedPerson);
```

This traverses the graph backwards, as you see in Figure 3-4.

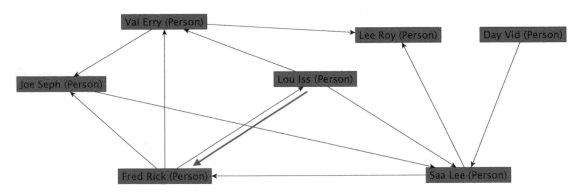

Figure 3-4. *Traversing the graph using a MATCH clause that fetches parent rows to Lou Iss*

As expected, the query returns

```
Person     Follows
---------  ----------
Fred Rick  Lou Iss
```

Starting at any given point of the graph is something you will use very frequently in the example code, particularly to find the child rows of a node and often to count or sum their data. In some cases, you will even start at every node and find the relationships to every other node.

Multiple MATCH Expressions

You started out with a simple MATCH expression, but you can do more than one MATCH expression in the same query. To make this easier to demonstrate, let's add new node type to the graph for programming language, as shown in Figure 3-5. The three new items are those with the lighter shade suffixed with ProgrammingLanguage. The edge, ProgramsWith, records when a person programs with a programming language. (I didn't name the edges on the diagram for clarity reasons.)

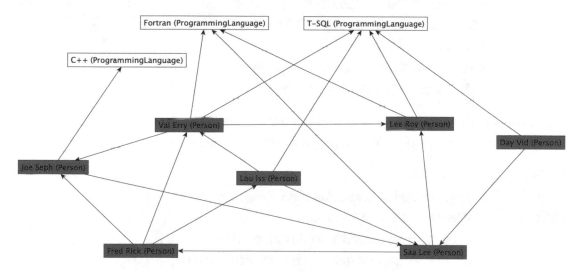

Figure 3-5. *Introducing ProgrammingLanguage to the example graph*

```
CREATE TABLE Network.ProgrammingLanguage
(
    Name nvarchar(30) NOT NULL
) AS NODE;

--load the node values
INSERT INTO Network.ProgrammingLanguage(Name)
```

```
VALUES('C++'),
      ('T-SQL'),
      ('Fortran');
```

Next, create the EDGE object. In this case, you won't add any columns, so the only columns in this object will be the ones from the graph database.

```
CREATE TABLE Network.ProgramsWith AS EDGE;
```

Just like before, add rows using two queries to the two different objects:

```
INSERT INTO Network.ProgramsWith($from_id, $to_id)
SELECT (SELECT $node_id
          FROM   Network.Person
          WHERE  FirstName = 'Lou'
            AND LastName = 'Iss') AS from_id,
       (SELECT $node_id
          FROM  Network.ProgrammingLanguage
          WHERE Name = 'T-SQL') as to_id;
```

The rest of the data loading statements are available in the download.

To start out, let's see people who program with a programming language:

```
SELECT      Person.Name AS Person,
            ProgrammingLanguage.Name AS ProgrammingLanguage
FROM        Network.Person AS Person,
            Network.ProgramsWith AS ProgramsWith,
            Network.ProgrammingLanguage AS ProgrammingLanguage
WHERE MATCH(Person-(ProgramsWith)->ProgrammingLanguage)
ORDER BY    Person.Name;
```

This returns

```
Person          ProgrammingLanguage
--------------- -------------------
Day Vid         T-SQL
Joe Seph        C++
Lee Roy         Fortran
Lee Roy         T-SQL
```

```
Lou Iss          T-SQL
Saa Lee          Fortran
Val Erry         Fortran
Val Erry         T-SQL
```

In Figure 3-5, you can see Val and Lee both have multiples, so they have multiple rows in the output. Fred does not have any languages linked, so he doesn't show up in the list. There is no way to make Fred show up in this list without adding a "not a programmer" node and link to it, or UNION ALL a query like

```
SELECT Person.Name AS PersonName,
       NULL AS ProgrammingLanguage
FROM   Network.Person
WHERE $node_id NOT IN (SELECT $from_id
                       FROM   Network.ProgramsWith);
```

This returns the row that has no programming language:

```
PersonName       ProgrammingLanguage
---------------  --------------------
Fred Rick        NULL
```

Now you can find the people who share a programming language ability by using a MATCH expressions. To do this, use two virtual copies of Person and two virtual copies of the edge (edges cannot be used more than one time in MATCH expressions, but tables can be reused if it makes sense.) Figure 3-6 shows the subgraph of ProgrammingLanguage nodes that Lou Iss is connected to and the other Person nodes that are connected to that language.

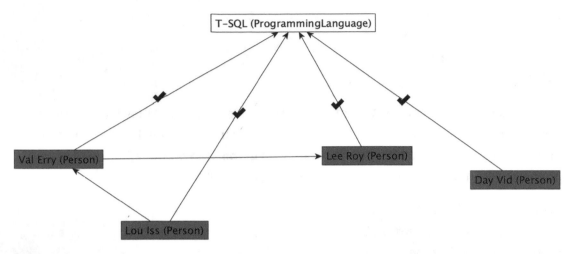

Figure 3-6. *Diagram showing the intersection of people who share a programming language skill with Lou Iss*

The following query implements this by essentially joining this set to itself with two filters. You join them together to get four output rows. You then filter out the row where Lou Iss matches Lou Iss, and you get three matches.

```
SELECT     Person.Name AS Person,
           Person2.Name AS Person2,
           ProgrammingLanguage.Name AS ProgrammingLanguage
FROM       Network.Person AS Person,
           Network.Person AS Person2,
           Network.ProgramsWith AS ProgramsWith,
           Network.ProgrammingLanguage AS ProgrammingLanguage,
           Network.ProgramsWith AS ProgramsWith2
WHERE MATCH(Person-(ProgramsWith)->ProgrammingLanguage)
     AND MATCH(Person2-(ProgramsWith2)->ProgrammingLanguage)
        --every person will match themselves
        AND Person2.PersonId <> Person.PersonId
        AND Person.Name = 'Lou Iss'
ORDER BY   Person.Name, Person2.Name;
```

The output of this query is as described (three rows):

```
Person          Person2     ProgrammingLanguage
-------------   -----------  -------------------

Lou Iss         Day Vid     T-SQL
Lou Iss         Lee Roy     T-SQL
Lou Iss         Val Erry    T-SQL
```

There are other formats of this MATCH expression you can use. In fact, you can express the two MATCH expressions for Person to ProgrammingLanguage in one ASCII art version of the query, like this:

```
WHERE MATCH(Person-(ProgramsWith)->ProgrammingLanguage<-
(ProgramsWith2)-Person2)
```

Another variation is that in the one MATCH expression, it expresses both sides of the equation. Finally, since you may not be able to combine everything into one MATCH expression like that, you can AND right in the MATCH expression:

```
WHERE   MATCH(Person-(ProgramsWith)->ProgrammingLanguage
            AND Person2-(ProgramsWith2)->ProgrammingLanguage)
```

And you can even pull in the Person to Person2 into the MATCH expression!

```
WHERE MATCH(Person2<-(Follows)-Person-
 (ProgramsWith)->ProgrammingLanguage<-(ProgramsWith2)-Person2)
```

Whether you want to cram everything into the one long ASCII art expression or not is a different discussion, as this can be a lot to handle (especially when troubleshooting a query that does not provide expected results).

In this next query, let's look for people who follow each other and share a programming language. These types of queries, with the generic many-to-many tables, are part of the great power of SQL graph objects.

```
SELECT      Person.Name AS Person,
            Person2.Name AS Person2,
            ProgrammingLanguage.Name
FROM        Network.Person AS Person,
            Network.Person AS Person2,
            Network.ProgramsWith AS ProgramsWith,
```

```
                Network.ProgrammingLanguage AS ProgrammingLanguage,
                Network.ProgramsWith AS ProgramsWith2,
                Network.Follows AS Follows
WHERE MATCH(Person-(ProgramsWith)->ProgrammingLanguage)
  AND MATCH(Person2-(ProgramsWith2)->ProgrammingLanguage)
AND MATCH(Person-(Follows)->Person2)
  AND Person2.PersonId <> Person.PersonId
  AND Person.Name = 'Lou Iss'
ORDER BY    Person, Person2, Name;
```

This filters the set down one more level, as you can see in Figure 3-7. Lou Iss only follows Val Erry among people in the subset of people that program with programming languages that Lou Iss also does.

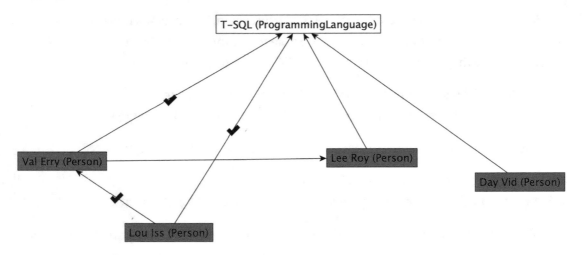

Figure 3-7. *Adding the extra follows relationship to your previous query*

The query returns the one person that Lou Iss follows who also programs with T-SQL:

```
Person          Person2          ProgrammingLanguage
-----------     -------------    ------------------------------
Lou Iss         Val Erry         T-SQL
```

You can use the multiple layers of MATCH expressions to tie your edges and nodes together to create rich queries to find how nodes are alike in multiple ways.

Traversing Variable Level Paths

So far, I have covered how to take one hop in the data structure. While the MATCH clause makes it easier to code the multiple connections, the power of a graph structure is quite often in querying longer paths to see how nodes are connected.

For example, say you want to find all the people in your graph subset that Day Vid is connected to on any level walk. There is only one direct connection from Day Vid to Saa Lee, but Saa is connected to several people, and in a third pass through the graph, Fred Rick is connected to three more people, as you can see in Figure 3-8.

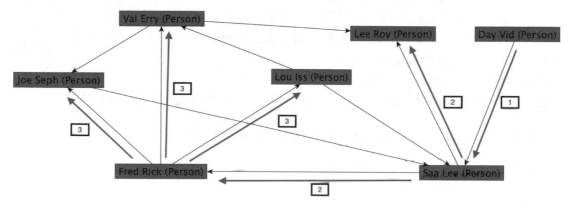

Figure 3-8. *Connections to all the people from Day Vid*

I stopped when every node had been touched. For example, I didn't continue from Val Erry to Joe Seph because Joe had already been reached. This is because we have the shortest walk/path from Day Vid to the Joe Seph already. And there is a path from Joe Seph to Saa Lee that would be a cycle. No cycle can ever go through our starting node, but there are always very likely to be cycles in the graph when the degree of the nodes is quite high (for example, Saa Lee has five connections, three incoming and two outgoing).

When you need to process your graph like this, SQL Server implements a SHORTEST_ PATH clause in the MATCH expression which is used to find (not surprisingly) a path from two nodes that is the shortest possible. It is a random (as far as we can tell) path because if there are multiple paths through the tree, it will pick just one. (This will be demonstrated again when I discuss how to process a weighted graph, which SQL Server does not implement in syntax as of SQL Server 2022.)

The syntax gets a little gnarly using SHORTEST_PATH, and some parts of the syntax took me quite a bit of work to learn. (I still have to look up the exact details every time I write a shortest path query and I am not ashamed to admit that!)

Displaying the Last Node in the Path

In this next query, you will do a minimal query to get the shortest path between the Lou Iss node to any other nodes that connect. After the query and results, I will break down the syntax.

```
SELECT Person.Name,
       LAST_VALUE(FollowedPerson.Name) WITHIN GROUP (GRAPH PATH)
                                       AS ConnectedPerson
FROM   Network.Person AS Person,
       Network.Follows FOR PATH AS Follows,
       Network.Person FOR PATH AS FollowedPerson
WHERE  Person.FirstName = 'Lou'
  AND Person.LastName = 'Iss'
  AND MATCH(SHORTEST_PATH(Person(-(Follows)->FollowedPerson)+));
```

The output of this query is every node other than Day Vid:

```
Person          ConnectedPerson
-------------   ---------------
Lou Iss         Val Erry
Lou Iss         Saa Lee
Lou Iss         Fred Rick
Lou Iss         Lee Roy
Lou Iss         Joe Seph
Lou Iss         Lou Iss
```

You can see in Figure 3-9 the different paths that are followed to get each value in the ConnectedPerson output. For example, Joe Seph is included because you can follow the path from Lou Iss to Val Erry and then Joe Seph.

To get that output, just walk through the graph and add each node that you find. On the first pass, you add Val Erry and Saa Lee. On the second, Lee Roy and Fred Rick, and so on. The output doesn't include any additional details, so just the node that you reach is all you need. There won't be any duplicates because you are finding the shortest path between nodes, and it only returns one of the paths if there are multiples.

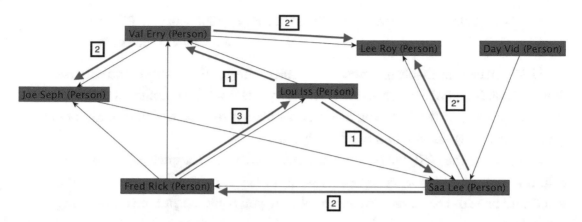

Figure 3-9. *Finding the shortest paths between Lou Iss and other nodes*

Note that Lou Iss' node is in the output, because on the third iteration of the breadth first algorithm it is reached.

In the query, a few new things are included. The first thing to look at is the FROM clause where you add FOR PATH to the edge and node objects that are used to calculate the path. The anchor object, in this case one of the copies of Network.Person, can be used in the query output directly, as with Person.Name in the output of the query. Objects with FOR PATH can only be used in graph aggregate functions, like the LAST_VALUE function.

```
FROM    Network.Person AS Person,
        Network.Follows FOR PATH AS Follows,
        Network.Person FOR PATH AS FollowedPerson
```

The MATCH expression has a bit more to it as well:

```
AND MATCH(SHORTEST_PATH(Person(-(Follows)->FollowedPerson)+));
```

You can see SHORTEST_PATH is inside the MATCH expression, and it in turn has an input of the anchor object and then the same sort of syntax for the objects in the path as before. The + indicates that you want all levels. You can specify how many levels to process with {1-N}. You always start with the first level, but then you can specify how far down the path to process. This can be essential when you have a huge graph to process and don't necessarily need to see items 1,000 hops away from your anchor node. The SHORTEST_PATH expression can be more complex (as I will demonstrate!) and you can include other MATCH criteria as well.

```
     LAST_VALUE(FollowedPerson.Name) WITHIN GROUP (GRAPH PATH)
                                              AS ConnectedPerson
```

LAST_VALUE is probably the most important of the graph functions you can use when doing a SHORTEST_PATH because the output is a value from the connected node. It is typically going to be the value you use to either display the piece of information to the user or fetch a key value to join to other objects.

You can use the LAST_VALUE function (and most others) in queries just as any column (though a lot more complex to display in the text of a book!). For example, if you didn't have the concatenated name column, you could output the name using this syntax:

```
CONCAT(
  LAST_VALUE(FollowedPerson.Firstname) WITHIN GROUP (GRAPH PATH),
  ' ',
  LAST_VALUE(FollowedPerson.LastName) WITHIN GROUP (GRAPH PATH))
                                              AS Name
```

Aggregation Along the Path

Now you have the basic concept down. (Trust me; it may take you a few times and a lot of tries to really get it to gel!) So let's look at some of the other functionality you can add to the output. You can do aggregates such as COUNT. COUNT is the standard way to get the number of hops between nodes. For example:

```
SELECT Person.Name AS Person,
       LAST_VALUE(FollowedPerson.Name) WITHIN GROUP
                              (GRAPH PATH) as ConnectedPerson,
       COUNT(FollowedPerson.PersonId) WITHIN GROUP
                              (GRAPH PATH) as Level
FROM   ... <same as before, for clarity>
```

When this is the SELECT clause, the COUNT aggregate counts each time there is a hop between a node. In the output, you can see that Val and Saa are directly connected to Lou, so one hop. Fred, Joe, and Lee are two. And it is three hops to get back to Lou.

```
Person           ConnectedPerson   Level
-------------    ---------------   -----------

Lou Iss          Val Erry          1
Lou Iss          Saa Lee           1
Lou Iss          Fred Rick         2
Lou Iss          Lee Roy           2
Lou Iss          Joe Seph          2
Lou Iss          Lou Iss           3
```

The next thing to add is the path that was actually taken to reach the LAST_VALUE value that is output. It is one of the most useful tools you have when debugging this code and displaying output to a user. The node labels of each node in the walk represented in the shortest path output.

This is done using STRING_AGG, and it demonstrates in the clearest manner how this algorithm is a breadth-first query. For each iteration, the FollowedPerson.Name value is added to the list (and only when there is another iteration does it include the '->' value because in the STRING_AGG function, the second parameter is the delimiter).

```
SELECT Person.Name,
       STRING_AGG(FollowedPerson.Name, '->') WITHIN GROUP
                                        (GRAPH PATH) AS Path
FROM...
```

The output from this query is

```
Name         Path
----------   --------------------------------

Lou Iss      Val Erry
Lou Iss      Saa Lee
Lou Iss      Saa Lee->Fred Rick
Lou Iss      Val Erry->Lee Roy
Lou Iss      Val Erry->Joe Seph
Lou Iss      Saa Lee->Fred Rick->Lou Iss
```

Note that the walk from Lou to Lee goes through Val only. On the diagram, it also goes through Saa. Later in in the chapter I will demonstrate how to include all walks in your output. (It will not be nearly as neat and tidy as these queries!)

In many cases, it shouldn't make much difference to your output what nodes are included in the chosen walk. That is, unless you start doing aggregates on the nodes in the path or want to choose among multiple paths. Then it gets a bit more complicated.

When I created the graph, I included value columns on each edge and node to let us see how they compare to the COUNT output since each value is 1.

```
SELECT STRING_AGG(FollowedPerson.Name, '->')WITHIN GROUP
                                (GRAPH PATH) AS PATH,
     COUNT(FollowedPerson.PersonId) WITHIN GROUP (GRAPH PATH)
                                AS Level,
     SUM(FollowedPerson.Value) WITHIN GROUP (GRAPH PATH)
                                AS SumNodeValues,
     SUM(Follows.Value) WITHIN GROUP (GRAPH PATH)
                                AS SumEdgeValues
FROM ...
```

The output of this query has two new columns that each have the same value as the level. You can see in the following output, where I added the extra values, that the sum doesn't include the base node:

Path	Level	SumNodeValues	SumEdgeValues
Val Erry	1	1	1
Saa Lee	1	1	1
Saa Lee->Fred Rick	2	2	2
Val Erry->Lee Roy	2	2	2
Val Erry->Joe Seph	2	2	2
Saa Lee->Fred Rick->Lou..	3	3	3

This is consistent with what you see in the path. You only see the nodes that are linked. And think about the edges to get to this location, for example Saa Lee->Fred Rick. There are two edges between Lou Iss and Fred Rick, so summing those values you get 2, as you see in the results. And there are two nodes in the chain after the base node. Again, be careful aggregating edges and intermediate nodes because the sum is based on the path taken, and other paths could have different values. It only makes sense if you are happy with the value of the random path chosen, which may be tricky to remember when looking at results.

For example, consider the subgraph in Figure 3-10. The direct path from Fred Rick to Saa Lee has the highest magnitude, but it is the only path you can choose using the SHORTEST_PATH syntax.

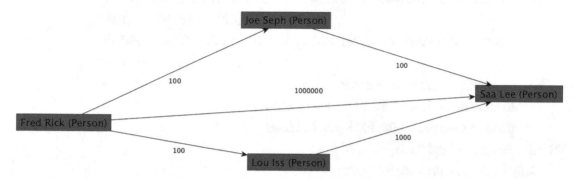

Figure 3-10. *Example subgraph with magnitude values on the edges*

Later in the chapter I will demonstrate how you can get the path in a different manner that is a lot more complex but will allow you to get every path between two nodes and compare them if desired.

Controlling Depth of Processing

In a very large graph, you probably don't want to traverse every level of the graph. For this reason, you sometimes need to limit the distance you will process. You control the number of levels to search in the SHORTEST_PATH syntax. In the previous examples, you used the following MATCH expression:

```
MATCH(SHORTEST_PATH(Person(-(Follows)->FollowedPerson)+))
```

The plus sign (+) in the syntax is where you control the iterations the processing will go. Change the + to {1,Depth} to control the depth. The 1 indicates the level you start at, but you can't start deeper in the hierarchy. If the first number is anything other than 1, you get the following error:

```
Msg 13942, Level 15, State 2, Line 556
The initial recursive quantifier must be 1: {1, ... }.
```

To show everyone linked at level 1 or 2, along with their path, you can use the following:

```
SELECT STRING_AGG(FollowedPerson.Name, '->') WITHIN GROUP
                                        (GRAPH PATH) AS Path,
        COUNT(FollowedPerson.PersonId) WITHIN GROUP (GRAPH PATH)
                                                        AS LEVEL
FROM    Network.Person AS Person,
        Network.Follows FOR PATH AS Follows,
        Network.Person FOR PATH AS FollowedPerson
WHERE   Person.FirstName = 'Lou'
    AND Person.LastName = 'Iss'
    AND MATCH(
            SHORTEST_PATH(Person(-(Follows)->FollowedPerson){1,2}));
```

The output of this query is

```
Path                     Level
------------------------ -----------
Val Erry                 1
Saa Lee                  1
Saa Lee->Fred Rick       2
Val Erry->Lee Roy        2
Val Erry->Joe Seph       2
```

You can see all the Level values are between 1 and 2. Re-execute the query with a + or even {1,3} and the difference you will see is one extra line with a Path of Saa Lee->Fred Rick->Lou Iss and a Level value of 3.

If you want to limit the levels on the lower end, like if you want to see levels 2 and 3, you need to use a CTE. With the grouping and such, you might think a HAVING clause would work, but it is not available.

```
WITH BaseRows AS (
SELECT STRING_AGG(FollowedPerson.Name, '->') WITHIN GROUP
                                        (GRAPH PATH) AS Path,
        COUNT(FollowedPerson.PersonId) WITHIN GROUP (GRAPH PATH)
                                                        AS LEVEL
FROM    Network.Person AS Person,
```

```
        Network.Follows FOR PATH AS Follows,
        Network.Person FOR PATH AS FollowedPerson
WHERE   Person.FirstName = 'Lou'
   AND Person.LastName = 'Iss'
   AND MATCH(
        SHORTEST_PATH(Person(-(Follows)->FollowedPerson){1,3})))
 )
SELECT *
FROM    BaseRows
WHERE   Level BETWEEN 2 AND 3;
```

The output of this query is the same as using +, but now the two rows with just one hop between your anchor node and the match have been filtered out.

Filtering for One Path

Several filters need to be handled in a common table expression (CTE). One that you will probably regularly use is filtering for the one path you are looking for. For example, say you want to see path Lou Iss to Lee Roy. You can filter the anchor node table to just one row, that of Lou Iss. The base query is put into a non-recursive CTE and then you filter the starting point in the query inside the CTE and the rows you want to see the match to in the outer query:

```
WITH BaseRows AS (
SELECT LAST_VALUE(FollowedPerson.Name) WITHIN GROUP (GRAPH PATH)
                                        AS ConnectedPerson,
       STRING_AGG(FollowedPerson.Name, '->') WITHIN GROUP
                                        (GRAPH PATH) AS Path
FROM    Network.Person AS Person,
        Network.Follows FOR PATH AS Follows,
        Network.Person FOR PATH AS FollowedPerson
WHERE   Person.FirstName = 'Lou'
   AND Person.LastName = 'Iss'
   AND MATCH(
        SHORTEST_PATH(Person(-(Follows)->FollowedPerson){1,3})))
 )
```

```
SELECT Path
FROM    BaseRows
WHERE ConnectedPerson = 'Lee Roy';
--probably ought to use a surrogate or name parts
--here in production code
```

The output of this query is just the path from Lou Iss to Lee Roy, which goes through Saa Lee:

```
Path
---------------------------
Saa Lee->Lee Roy
```

Finding All Paths Between Nodes

The following code is about as messy as it gets in this book. The basic query pattern will be repeated a few times in later chapters because it is an essential skill. But it absolutely is messy to do.

The idea is that you implement the basic query that Microsoft has built using SHORTEST_PATH, but with a twist. You don't stop processing for anything except a cycle in the structure.

Using the current graph, if you want to find all the paths between two nodes, you can use the following code. I include comments in the code where useful to point out how the code works. But the idea is that using a recursive CTE, you keep iterating on the set using a breadth-first algorithm, but you keep every branch of the output, even when you find the node in the query. You filter the output later in the process.

```
--fetch the starting point
DECLARE @FirstName NVARCHAR(100) = N'Lou';
DECLARE @LastName NVARCHAR(100) = N'Iss';

--filter for the ending point
DECLARE @ToFirstName NVARCHAR(100) = N'Lee';
DECLARE @ToLastName NVARCHAR(100) = N'Roy';

--for larger graphs, this may be need to
--stop excessive recursion
DECLARE @MaxLevel INT =10;
```

```
WITH BaseRows
AS (
    --the CTE anchor is just the starting node
    SELECT Person.PersonId,
           Person.PersonId AS FollowsPersonId,
           Person.Name,
        --the path that contains the readable path we have
        --built in all examples with the anchor included
           CAST(Person.Name AS NVARCHAR(4000)) AS Path,
        --this path is use to stop loops. If the personId is
        --found in the path already, then the recursion
        --will stop
           CAST(CONCAT('\', Person.PersonId, '\')
                               AS VARCHAR(8000)) AS IdPath,
           0 AS level --the level
    FROM Network.Person
    WHERE Person.FirstName = @FirstName --Here's where you filter
          AND Person.LastName = @LastName --the anchor
    UNION ALL
    --pretty typical 1 level graph query:
    SELECT Person.PersonId AS PersonId,
           FollowedPerson.PersonId AS FollowsPersonId,
           FollowedPerson.Name,
           BaseRows.Path + '>' + FollowedPerson.Name,
           BaseRows.IdPath +
           CAST(FollowedPerson.PersonId AS VARCHAR(10)) + '\',
           BaseRows.level + 1
    FROM Network.Person,
         Network.Follows,
         Network.Person AS FollowedPerson,
         BaseRows
    WHERE MATCH(Person-(Follows)->FollowedPerson)
      --this joins the anchor to the recursive part of the query
      AND BaseRows.FollowsPersonId = Person.PersonId
    --this is the part that stops recursion, treating the
      --string value like an array
```

69

```
        AND NOT BaseRows.IdPath LIKE CONCAT('%\',
                                    FollowedPerson.PersonId, '\%')
            AND BaseRows.level <= @MaxLevel)

SELECT BaseRows.Path
FROM BaseRows
WHERE BaseRows.Name = 'Lee Roy';
```

The output of this query is (I manually added a number to correspond to Figure 3-11)

```
   Path
   ------------------------------------------------

1  Lou Iss>Val Erry>Lee Roy
2  Lou Iss>Val Erry>Joe Seph>Saa Lee>Lee Roy
3  Lou Iss>Saa Lee>Lee Roy
4  Lou Iss>Saa Lee>Fred Rick>Val Erry>Lee Roy
```

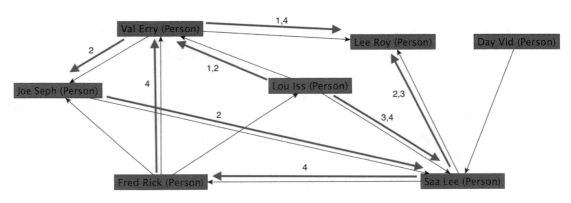

Figure 3-11. *Tracing the paths from Lou Iss to Lee Roy in the sample graph*

You can trace the various paths on Figure 3-11.

Even in this fairly small example, you can see that what would be one result found in two iteration steps has expanded to four, with an extra step.

This sort of solution will be necessary if your user wants to answer questions like, is there a path between Lou Iss and Lee Roy that also includes Fred Rick? There is no trivial way to answer this question in most cyclic graphs because the structure is entirely unpredictable. For a directed graph, it could be easier (and far easier for a tree), but if you need to be very specific in your path, expect that processing is going to be more complicated.

Weighted Graph Calculations

In the previous section, you looked at finding all the paths between two nodes. This is essential to the process of doing weighted graph calculations. For the example code in this chapter, you simply use the graph we created with the values that were established (all the values were 1 for simplicity).

In the following code, I highlight how it differs from the query in the previous section, "Finding All Paths Between Nodes:"

```
DECLARE @FirstName NVARCHAR(100) = N'Lou';
DECLARE @LastName NVARCHAR(100) = N'Iss';

DECLARE @ToFirstName NVARCHAR(100) = N'Lee';
DECLARE @ToLastName NVARCHAR(100) = N'Roy';

DECLARE @MaxLevel INT = 10;

WITH BaseRows
AS (SELECT Person.PersonId,
           Person.PersonId AS FollowsPersonId,
           Person.Name,
           CAST(Person.Name AS NVARCHAR(4000)) AS Path,
           CAST(CONCAT('\', Person.PersonId, '\') AS VARCHAR(8000))
AS IdPath,
           0 AS level,
           0 AS WeightedCost, --edge sums
           Person.Value AS NodeSum --node sums
    FROM Network.Person
    WHERE Person.FirstName = @FirstName
          AND Person.LastName = @LastName
    UNION ALL
    SELECT Person.PersonId AS PersonId,
           FollowedPerson.PersonId AS FollowsPersonId,
           FollowedPerson.Name,
           BaseRows.Path + '>' + FollowedPerson.Name,
           BaseRows.IdPath + CAST(FollowedPerson.PersonId AS
VARCHAR(10)) + '\',
```

```
                BaseRows.level + 1,

                --add the values in each iteration
                --Edge Values (1 less value than nodes)
                BaseRows.WeightedCost + Follows.Value,
                --Nodes, including anchor
                BaseRows.NodeSum + FollowedPerson.Value
        FROM Network.Person,
             Network.Follows,
             Network.Person AS FollowedPerson,
             BaseRows
        WHERE MATCH(Person-(Follows)->FollowedPerson)
                    AND BaseRows.FollowsPersonId = Person.PersonId
                    AND NOT BaseRows.IdPath LIKE CONCAT('%\', FollowedPerson.
PersonId, '\%')
                    AND BaseRows.level < 10)
SELECT BaseRows.Path,
       BaseRows.WeightedCost,
       BaseRows.NodeSum
FROM BaseRows
WHERE BaseRows.Name = 'Lee Roy';
```

The output of this query is

Path	WeightedCost	NodeSum
Lou Iss>Val Erry>Lee Roy	2	3
Lou Iss>Val Erry>Joe Seph>Saa Lee>Lee Roy	4	5
Lou Iss>Saa Lee>Lee Roy	2	3
Lou Iss>Saa Lee>Fred Rick>Val Erry>Lee Roy	4	5

Since every node and edge had a value of 1, you can see the costs and sum are basically the same as a count of nodes and edges that were touched processing the path. If you want to do different aggregates, you need to create that code yourself. So, for an average, keep the sum and count to do the average in the output query. For a MIN- or MAX-like output, you need to compare the value in every iteration.

With this table, you could easily alter the query to get the cheapest or most expensive path using a TOP 1 (or TOP 1 WITH TIES if you want to see all the items that tied). So, say you want the shortest paths, you can change the query using the CTE to

```
SELECT TOP 1 WITH TIES BaseRows.Path,
       BaseRows.WeightedCost,
       BaseRows.NodeSum
FROM   BaseRows
WHERE  BaseRows.Name = 'Lee Roy'
ORDER BY BaseRows.WeightedCost ASC;
```

You results would be just the first two line of the results of the previous query.

Checking Conditions on the Matched Item

Finding all the nodes that you can find a path to is just the first step in a lot of queries. Sometimes you want to find all the people that you connect with on some level that has some characteristic.

As an example, say Lou Iss is looking for someone they are connected with who programs in C++. You can do this in two steps, get everyone that Lou Iss is connected to and then take those items (maybe in a temp table or CTE) and find their matches in the ProgramsWith edge. Figure 3-12 shows this, with boxes around the nodes that Lou Iss has a connection to on some level, and then indicated the one node that has a connection to C++.

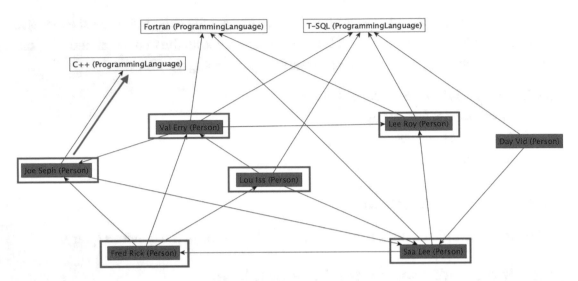

Figure 3-12. *Nodes in the graph that have a relationship to Lou Iss and also to C++*

Using the LAST_NODE extension on the MATCH syntax, you can do that in one (relatively) simple query. In the following query, I highlighted the syntax that lets us take the nodes returned by the shortest path and then connect them to ProgrammingLanguage nodes:

```
SELECT   LAST_VALUE(FollowedPerson.Name)
            WITHIN GROUP (GRAPH PATH) AS ConnectedPerson,
        STRING_AGG(FollowedPerson.Name, '->')
            WITHIN GROUP (GRAPH PATH) AS Path
FROM    Network.Person AS Person,
        Network.Follows FOR PATH AS Follows,
        Network.Person FOR PATH AS FollowedPerson,
        Network.ProgramsWith AS ProgramsWith,
        Network.ProgrammingLanguage
WHERE   Person.FirstName = 'Lou'
    AND Person.LastName = 'Iss'
    AND MATCH(SHORTEST_PATH(Person(-(Follows)->FollowedPerson)+)
            --Note, this is valid syntax. The -> can be on a
            --different line
            AND LAST_NODE(FollowedPerson)-(ProgramsWith)
                            ->ProgrammingLanguage)
    AND ProgrammingLanguage.NAME = 'C++';
```

This returns

```
ConnectedPerson     Path
----------------    -----------------------
Joe Seph            Val Erry->Joe Seph
```

Note a few things. First, even though `Network.ProgramsWith` and `Network.ProgrammingLanguage` are used in the query with `SHORTEST_PATH` and they are not the anchor table, you do not use `FOR PATH` because their part of the query does not use the path. Putting `FOR PATH` behind either of the programming objects will result in an error such as

```
Msg 13949, Level 16, State 2, Line 929
The table name or alias 'ProgramsWith' was marked as FOR PATH but was not
used in the recursive section of a SHORTEST_PATH clause.
```

The `LAST_NODE` graph function gives you a reference to the graph structures in the last node of the `SHORTEST_PATH`. It is similar to `LAST_VALUE`, but node gives you a reference instead of a value. From there you can look for matches, and you can design some complex queries to answer some very complex questions for your users.

Summary

In this chapter, you looked at the basics of the syntax to create and query data in SQL Server's graph tables. There are many differences and similarities to typical relational tables, but there are a lot of differences that you need to know to use these objects.

You learned about creating the objects and then how to load new data in the tables in the simplest manner. In the next chapter, I will extend both of these topics, including how to protect your objects from bad data and ways to make loading data easier.

After creating some data, you looked at most of the syntax needed to query the data in your graph tables. The syntax centers on the `MATCH` expression along with the `SHORTEST_PATH` extension for querying for data at multiple levels in the graph.

All of these topics are fundamental to most of the graphs you will be creating and querying throughout the book.

CHAPTER 4

SQL Graph Tables: Extended Topics

In Chapter 3, I presented the basics of using SQL Server's graph tables. In many ways they resemble typical SQL Server tables with rows and columns, SELECT statements to access data, and such. But some parts were way different, especially how the internal graph database is structured. Working with pseudo-columns maybe a new concept, unless you have worked with partitioning (and their use in partitioning is not as user facing as using $node_id, $from_id, etc.).

In this chapter, I am going to go beyond the basics and give you tools to build interfaces and protect your data using constraints, indexes, and triggers. You will also delve into the metadata that you will often need to inspect when you get a SQL Server database and want to know what graph tables exist and details about them.

The goal of this chapter is to finish setting up all the techniques you will be using in the last half of the book to demonstrate building useful databases with SQL Server graph objects.

The database you will be using for this chapter is the same one in the same state as it was left in Chapter 3. If you are starting with this chapter (to refresh the skills I cover in this chapter, there is a backup file in the downloads named https://github.com/Apress/practical-graph-structures that will let you create the database exactly how it should be when you start this chapter.).

Advanced Data Creation Techniques

In this section, I show two techniques that go beyond what was covered in Chapter 1. If you are building interfaces where you load more than one row at a time, these techniques will help you load data into your graph objects in a quicker manner.

L. Davidson, *Practical Graph Structures in SQL Server and Azure SQL*, https://doi.org/10.1007/978-1-4842-9459-8_4

First, I introduce an interface layer that lets you insert data into a view using regular key values from your tables. This is done using an instead of a trigger object to do the graph DB translation work for you.

The second section shows you how to insert data directly into the graph columns using composable JSON tags. This way you can use existing data you have for the id values. rather than letting SQL Server dictate what the values will be and then having to look them up again.

Building an Interface Layer

In the previous chapter, all examples of creating edge data followed the same basic pattern:

```
INSERT INTO Network.Follows($from_id, $to_id)
--look up the $from_id
SELECT (    SELECT Person.$node_id
        FROM    Network.Person
        WHERE   Person.FirstName = 'Fred'
            AND Person.LastName = 'Rick') AS from_id,
        --just a name to make it easier to see when debugging
    --look up a to_id
    (    SELECT Person.$node_id
        FROM    Network.Person
        WHERE   Person.FirstName = 'Joe'
            AND Person.LastName = 'Seph') AS to_id;
```

You look up the two $node_id values in two subqueries, which together would form a $from_id, $to_id pair, and then insert the values. This is the pattern you will likely use when loading a single row in a procedure, but it is cumbersome if you want to load thousands of rows or want to translate one of your relational databases into a graph for analysis and you don't have an integer key to work with. (More on that in a later section on composable JSON tags.)

INSERT

In this section, you are going to build an interface that allows you to insert the same data using the natural key values:

```
INSERT INTO Network.Follows (FromFirstName, FromLastName,
            ToFirstName, ToLastName)
VALUES ('Fred', 'Rick','Joe', 'Seph')
```

This method uses a view object with an INSTEAD OF trigger object to allow the looking up of the $from_id and $to_id to happen internally.

Note   For these examples, you will be using the Name column to simplify the code for the book. When you load lots of data, always try to use a value that has an index to join on.

For this example, create another schema that is there to support user interfaces for the data called NetworkUI:

```
IF SCHEMA_ID('Network_UI') IS NULL
    EXEC ('CREATE SCHEMA Network_UI');
```

The view you create will only feasibly let you insert data in one specific node table to another specific node table using one specific key (primary or alternate). So, you need to repeat this process for each relationship you wish to use this technique with.

In your case, you are going to implement the relationship between Network. Person to Network.Person through the Network.Follows edge. The basic view is straightforward. It's just a query of the table returning the two key values from your nodes that you want to present to the user. It is completely up to your needs if you want to use a natural or surrogate key. The only requirement is that you present the user with values that will uniquely identify the relationship between two rows that they can know the value of.

If you want to be able to type your INSERT statement manually with keys you know, use the natural key. For this example, use the surrogate keys to match the data in the source data.

This is the code for the view:

```
CREATE OR ALTER VIEW Network_UI.Person_Follows_Person
AS
SELECT Person.PersonId AS PersonId,
       FollowedPerson.PersonId AS FollowsPersonId,
       Follows.Value AS Value
```

```
FROM Network.Person,
     Network.Follows,
     Network.Person AS FollowedPerson
WHERE MATCH(Person-(Follows)->FollowedPerson);
```

Execute the following query using the view:

```
SELECT Person_Follows_Person.PersonId,
       Person_Follows_Person.FollowsPersonId,
       Person_Follows_Person.Value
FROM   Network_UI.Person_Follows_Person;
```

The output looks like this (just showing the first 3 rows of 11):

```
PersonId    FollowsPersonId Value
----------- --------------- -----------
1           6               1
1           2               1
6           5               1
```

Now you are going to create an INSTEAD OF trigger object that will take these three columns as input and translate them to the internal graph identifier values. Then using the graph values, you insert the rows into the table. This makes it a lot easier to load lots of data into a table without dealing with all the translation to graph key values. It especially makes ad-hoc inserts easier because you never have to find the internal values.

Note   Some of the examples in this section don't look like you are saving all that much work, since you are going to have to look up the regular key just like the graph values. This technique will become especially useful when taking a regular many-to-many relationship and translating it to a graph edge.

```
CREATE OR ALTER TRIGGER Network_UI.Person_FollowsPerson_$InsteadOfInsertTrigger
ON Network_UI.Person_Follows_Person
INSTEAD OF INSERT
AS
SET NOCOUNT ON;
```

```
--If you add more code, you should add error handling code.
BEGIN
 INSERT INTO Network.Follows($from_id, $to_id, Value)
 SELECT Person.$node_id, FollowedPerson.$node_id,
            inserted.Value
 FROM Inserted
     JOIN Network.Person
         ON Person.PersonId = Inserted.PersonId
     JOIN Network.Person AS FollowedPerson
         ON FollowedPerson.PersonId = Inserted.FollowsPersonId;
END;
```

Using the Network_UI.Person_Follows_Person view, you can write quick queries using regular joins with the key values. For example, you can join the view back to the Network.Person to get the names like this:

```
SELECT Person.Name, FollowedPerson.Name AS FollowedPerson
FROM    Network_UI.Person_Follows_Person as Follows
         JOIN Network.Person
            ON Person.PersonId = Follows.PersonId
         JOIN Network.Person AS FollowedPerson
            ON FollowedPerson.PersonId = Follows.FollowsPersonId
WHERE   Person.Name = 'Lou Iss';
```

Take care because while this will be fast on your small data set, you may need to do some tuning of your queries. Use the MATCH expression and your graph tables as often as possible. Execute this query, and you will get the following result:

```
Name                FollowedPerson
----------------- ----------------------

Lou Iss           Saa Lee
Lou Iss           Val Erry
```

If you look at the query plan for the execution of the query in SSMS, you will see something similar to Figure 4-1.

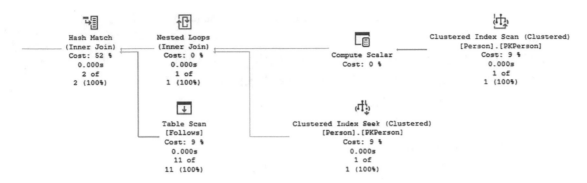

Figure 4-1. *Partial query plan showing that you are joining the Person table to the Follows table. The rest of the query plan would show another hash join to Person*

Looking at the query plan, you will notice a HASH JOIN operator for the query with the edge object. Later in the chapter, you will look at adding indexes to your node and edge objects to possibly improve performance (note that smaller data sets like you are working with now may have very naïve plans generated for queries that will change as data sets grow).

While there is a lot different in how you work with node and edge objects, there are a lot of similarities too, and you will need to take some control over performance tuning based on how you use your objects. As noted, using this view isn't a big value for querying, but if you had a table of the id values to turn into a graph, it would rock.

To demonstrate, insert a row using the surrogate key values found by running these queries:

```
SELECT Person.PersonId  AS PersonId
 FROM Network.Person
 WHERE Person.Name = 'Lou iss';
```

```
SELECT Person.PersonId  AS FollowsPersonId
FROM Network.Person
WHERE Person.Name = 'Joe Seph';
```

Take the values returned and use them in the following query. For the sample set, the values are 2 and 6. So you could insert the new row using the following statement:

```
INSERT INTO Network_UI.Person_Follows_Person
     (PersonId,FollowsPersonId,Value)
VALUES (2, 6, 10);
```

Execute the following query:

```
SELECT Person.Name, FollowsPerson.Name AS FollowedPerson
FROM   Network.Person, Network.Follows,
       Network.Person AS FollowsPerson
WHERE MATCH(Person-(Follows)->FollowsPerson)
 AND Person.Name = 'Lou Iss';
```

You will see that a row with Joe Seph as the followed person is now in the result set.

UPDATE

As I said earlier in the book, edge objects cannot have their $from_id or $to_id values updated. And this makes good sense. But let's say you want to update the value to be 1, to match all your other data.

```
UPDATE Network_UI.Person_Follows_Person
SET Person_Follows_Person.Value = 1
WHERE PersonId = (SELECT Person.PersonId
                    FROM Network.Person
                    WHERE Person.Name = 'Lou iss')
AND Person_Follows_Person.FollowsPersonId =
                    (SELECT Person.PersonId
                     FROM Network.Person
                     WHERE Person.Name = 'Joe Seph');
```

This works great because you are only updating data from one table in your update. Any attempt to change the key values along with the value will fail as

```
UPDATE Network_UI.Person_Follows_Person
SET Person_Follows_Person.Value = 1,
    Person_Follows_Person.PersonId = 0
```

returns an error:

```
Msg 4405, Level 16, State 1, Line 85
View or function 'Network_UI.Person_Follows_Person' is not updatable
because the modification affects multiple base tables.
```

If you just try to update one key value, which is in only one table, like this

```
UPDATE Network_UI.Person_Follows_Person
SET Person_Follows_Person.PersonId = 0;
```

it does try, but the value links back to the identity value of the Network.Person object, so you get this error:

```
Msg 8102, Level 16, State 1, Line 105
Cannot update identity column 'PersonId'.
```

If you desire to update the $from_id and $to_id values, it is doable in an instead-of trigger object (requiring a delete and an insert, which should definitely have more involved error handling if you are building your production code), but I only suggest this when you are creating tables to work with in an ad-hoc manner. Just have your code do the delete and insert. This is an operation that will be used when you implement a tree as reparenting a node is a common operation, which technically changes the relationship.

Note   In the downloads for Chapter 4, there is a code generator to generate a view and INSTEAD OF trigger objects for you. It includes an update one named InterfaceViewCodeGenerator.sql. The code is documented and although there are a lot of settings needed, it will generate the basic framework for the entire interface.

DELETE

Delete operations using natural keys may make perfect sense depending on your application (especially when users manipulate data manually). Deletes using the user interface tables also need a trigger to translate the id values to the key of the edge rows.

```
DELETE FROM Network_UI.Person_Follows_Person
WHERE PersonId = (SELECT Person.PersonId
                   FROM Network.Person
                   WHERE Person.Name = 'Lou iss')
AND Person_Follows_Person.FollowsPersonId =
                  (SELECT Person.PersonId
                   FROM Network.Person
                   WHERE Person.Name = 'Joe Seph');
```

Just as with the update before, you get the same Error 4405. So, let's build a simple INSTEAD OF DELETE trigger object. The weird question here is, what will the deleted columns contain? Because unlike the insert trigger, where you provide the values, in this next trigger the query will be executed. So, to start with, you will just return the rows from the deleted object in a query.

```
CREATE OR ALTER TRIGGER Network_UI.Person_Follows_
Person$InsteadOfDeleteTrigger
ON Network_UI.Person_Follows_Person
INSTEAD OF DELETE
AS
SET NOCOUNT ON;
--If you add more code, you should add error handling code.
BEGIN
    SELECT *
    FROM Deleted;
END;
```

> **Note**   If this doesn't work for you, check the settings noted in this article: https://learn.microsoft.com/sql/database-engine/configure-windows/disallow-results-from-triggers-server-configuration-option. It is clearly best to not have results from normal triggers, but it is very useful in a development case to be able to see what is being output.

Execute the following statement and you will see that the deleted table contains the data from the view, since the trigger's main code is simply to return the contents of the deleted virtual table:

```
DELETE FROM Network_UI.Person_Follows_Person
WHERE PersonId = (    SELECT Person.PersonId
                      FROM   Network.Person
                      WHERE  Person.Name = 'Lou iss')
   AND Person_Follows_Person.FollowsPersonId =
                  (    SELECT Person.PersonId
                       FROM   Network.Person
                       WHERE  Person.Name = 'Joe Seph');
```

This returns the following, showing that the deleted table looks just like you expect based on the structure of the view:

```
PersonId     FollowsPersonId Value
-----------  --------------- -----------
2            6               1
```

So, you can write the trigger just like this:

```
CREATE OR ALTER TRIGGER Network_UI.Person_Follows_
Person$InsteadOfDeleteTrigger
ON Network_UI.Person_Follows_Person
INSTEAD OF DELETE
AS
SET NOCOUNT ON;
 --If you add more code, you should add error handling code.
 BEGIN
  DELETE FROM Network.Follows --<The real table
  FROM Network.Person, Network.Follows,
       Network.Person AS FollowedPerson,
          Deleted
  --MATCH, then join to deleted to reduce the set to
  --rows being deleted.
  WHERE MATCH(Person-(Follows)->FollowedPerson)
    and  deleted.PersonId = Person.PersonId
    and  deleted.FollowsPersonId = FollowedPerson.PersonId
 END;
```

Now you can delete the data in a straightforward manner as if it was not a table that had special columns internally:

```
DELETE FROM Network_UI.Person_Follows_Person
WHERE Person_Follows_Person.PersonId = 2
  AND Person_Follows_Person.FollowsPersonId = 6;
```

After deleting in the rows, you can see the row is gone. Be sure and test with creating and deleting multiple rows when you build triggers.

```
SELECT  Person.Name AS PersonName,
        FollowedPerson.Name AS FollowsPersonName
FROM    Network.Person,
        Network.Follows,
        Network.Person AS FollowedPerson
WHERE   MATCH(Person-(Follows)->FollowedPerson)
  AND   Person.Name = 'Lou Iss';
```

Loading Data Using Composable JSON Tags

For this next section, you are going to change to a different, publicly available database called AdventureWorksLT. I used the 2019 version available on Microsoft's Learn site here: https://learn.microsoft.com/sql/samples/adventureworks-install-configure. Use the LT version because it has integer key values which make this process a lot easier. If you were loading data from a database with GUID key values, or even multi-part key values, you would create staging tables in tempdb with an identity key value to map to temporarily (and make a table with sourceKey, identityKey to load from the source table). I leave that to you, dear reader, as it isn't terribly hard, but it definitely will make reading the example code harder.

Ok, once you have that database restored, create a simple graph of Customer-Purchased->Product from the data. Include a Label column for each node and a purchase date on the edge. Don't put a uniqueness constraint on the edge because the goal is primarily to show the loading method.

First, create a new schema to hold your new objects:

```
CREATE SCHEMA SalesGraph;
```

Next, you are going to create the node table objects. In these objects you will include the surrogate key from the relational table, which is useful for fetching additional information after you have fetched a set of data. You can tune the amount of data you need in your graph tables to your needs if you are putting the graph in the same database with a relational copy of the data.

```
CREATE TABLE SalesGraph.Customer
(
    CustomerId int NOT NULL
        CONSTRAINT PKCustomer PRIMARY KEY,
```

```
        Label nvarchar(100) NOT NULL
                CONSTRAINT AKCustomer UNIQUE
) AS NODE;

CREATE TABLE SalesGraph.Product
(
        ProductId int NOT NULL
                CONSTRAINT PKProduct PRIMARY KEY,
        Label nvarchar(100) NOT NULL
                CONSTRAINT AKProduct UNIQUE
) AS NODE;
```

Next, the edge is created. In the edge, the key from the table in the database where it came from is included, along with the time the item was purchased, which can definitely be useful in your analysis.

```
CREATE TABLE SalesGraph.Purchased
(
        SalesOrderDetailId int NOT NULL
                    CONSTRAINT AKPurchased UNIQUE,
        PurchaseTime datetime2(0) NOT NULL
) AS EDGE;
```

You could simply just fetch the rows as they exist in the source data, do a little bit of transformation, and load the data with a simple insert statement:

```
--customerID added to label for uniqueness... why there
--is duplication is beyond this exercise's needs
INSERT INTO SalesGraph.Customer WITH (TABLOCKX)
(
    CustomerId, Label
)
SELECT CustomerID,
       CONCAT(FirstName, ' ', LastName, ' ', CustomerID) AS Label
FROM SalesLT.Customer
ORDER BY Label;
```

Looking at a few rows of the output, you see

```
SELECT TOP 2
       $node_id,
       CustomerId
FROM SalesGraph.Customer;
```

The id values are 0 and 1 for the first two rows:

```
$node_id_06C54C432DE544E8995B29AFDAD55455
-----------------------------------------------------------------
{"type":"node","schema":"SalesGraph","table":"Customer","id":0}
{"type":"node","schema":"SalesGraph","table":"Customer","id":1}

CustomerId
-----------
202
29943
```

The id values don't match the CustomerId column values. In some respects, this is a good thing. You almost never want to be using the $node_id values for any purpose, but when loading edge rows, if you could predict the values, you wouldn't need to look them up, letting you load data far faster.

Luckily, you can compose the JSON yourself, and Microsoft has provided you the tools to do so as part of the graph functionality. Assuming you are loading in copies of data (possibly for analysis, possibly for a first-time load), and that you don't use values approaching max bigint (a very large number indeed), then you can save a lot of processing time using the following technique. I regularly use this technique for sample data because I can load a database with different datasets very quickly. To show this, start by truncating the data in the SalesGraph.Customer table.

```
TRUNCATE TABLE SalesGraph.Customer;
```

The NODE_ID_FROM_PARTS function takes an object_id for the node table and an integer that will become the graph id value. The following query shows you that the CustomerId now matches the graph id. The object_id that you pass in must match an object_id in the graph tables or the output will be null, so you cannot manufacture bad data using this method:

```
SELECT NODE_ID_FROM_PARTS(OBJECT_ID('SalesGraph.Customer'),
                                                CustomerID),
       CustomerID,
       CONCAT(FirstName, ' ', LastName, ' ', CustomerID) AS LABEL
FROM SalesLT.Customer;
```

Look at the output and you will see that the data matches surrogate key to surrogate key:

```
----------------------------------------------------------------
{"type":"node","schema":"SalesGraph","table":"Customer","id":1}
{"type":"node","schema":"SalesGraph","table":"Customer","id":2}
{"type":"node","schema":"SalesGraph","table":"Customer","id":3}
CustomerId  Label
-----------  ----------------------
1           Orlando Gee 1
2           Keith Harris 2
3           Donna Carreras 3
```

Now you can insert values into the $node_id column along with the other two columns:

```
INSERT INTO SalesGraph.Customer
(
    $Node_id, CustomerId,Label
)
SELECT NODE_ID_FROM_PARTS(OBJECT_ID('SalesGraph.Customer'),
                                                CustomerID),
       CustomerID,
       CONCAT(FirstName, ' ', LastName, ' ', CustomerID) AS LABEL
FROM SalesLT.Customer;
```

Next, do the same for the product (same duplicate name concern as for the customer so add the ProductId as a suffix):

```
INSERT INTO SalesGraph.Product
(
    $Node_id, ProductId, Label
)
```

```
SELECT NODE_ID_FROM_PARTS(OBJECT_ID('SalesGraph.Product'),
                                              ProductID),
       ProductID,
       CONCAT(Name, ' ', ProductID) AS LABEL
FROM SalesLT.Product;
```

Now run the following query that gets you the customer and product that was purchased by joining through the SalesLT.SalesOrderHeader table:

```
SELECT SalesOrderDetail.SalesOrderDetailID,
       OrderDate AS PurchaseTime,
       ProductID,
       CustomerID
FROM SalesLT.SalesOrderHeader
   JOIN SalesLT.SalesOrderDetail
      ON SalesOrderHeader.SalesOrderID =
                     SalesOrderDetail.SalesOrderID;
```

Now you can create the data in the SalesGraph.Purchased edge table with the composed JSON values, referencing the tables where you loaded the node data:

```
 INSERT INTO SalesGraph.Purchased
(
    SalesOrderDetailId, PurchaseTime,
       $from_id,$to_id
)
SELECT SalesOrderDetail.SalesOrderDetailID,
       OrderDate AS PurchaseTime,
       NODE_ID_FROM_PARTS(OBJECT_ID('SalesGraph.Customer'),
                                              CustomerID),
       NODE_ID_FROM_PARTS(OBJECT_ID('SalesGraph.Product'),
                                              ProductID)
FROM SalesLT.SalesOrderHeader
   JOIN SalesLT.SalesOrderDetail
      ON SalesOrderHeader.SalesOrderID = SalesOrderDetail.SalesOrderID;
```

Finally, execute this SQL and you can see all the data you have loaded:

```
SELECT Customer.Label, Product.Label
FROM   SalesGraph.Customer,
       SalesGraph.Purchased,
       SalesGraph.Product
WHERE MATCH(Customer-(Purchased)->Product)
```

One note: The graph queries you created to insert data can be executed in any order (or simultaneously for larger loads). Missing parent node data causes confusing queries, but it is not illegal. For example, clear out the SalesGraph.Customer and SalesGraph. Product objects:

```
TRUNCATE TABLE SalesGraph.Customer;
TRUNCATE TABLE SalesGraph.Product;
```

Then rerun the SELECT statement with the MATCH clause you just executed. You still get the same number of rows, but now all the label values are NULL. After initially loading the data with your own key values, it is highly suggested to add an edge constraint to clean up/prevent dangling references (this will be covered later in this chapter).

If you truncate the data in the SalesGraph.Purchased object, things will be cleaned up. But note that you can run the INSERT statement that creates the edge rows only and it does not validate that the id values are valid. The main validation done is to check to see that the object_id value used in the $node_id values are real.

While you can create edge rows without related node rows, the node table does need to exist. As the final example in this section, truncate the edge and drop the two node tables. Then go ahead and drop the customer and product tables.

```
TRUNCATE TABLE SalesGraph.Purchased;
DROP TABLE IF EXISTS SalesGraph.Customer, SalesGraph.Product;
```

Now if you try to insert the data into the edge as

```
INSERT INTO SalesGraph.Purchased
(
    SalesOrderDetailId,
    PurchaseTime,
    $from_id,
    $to_id
)
```

```
SELECT SalesOrderDetail.SalesOrderDetailID,
       OrderDate AS PurchaseTime,
       NODE_ID_FROM_PARTS(OBJECT_ID('SalesGraph.Customer'),
                                        CustomerID),
       NODE_ID_FROM_PARTS(OBJECT_ID('SalesGraph.Product'),
                                        ProductID)
FROM SalesLT.SalesOrderHeader
    JOIN SalesLT.SalesOrderDetail
        ON SalesOrderHeader.SalesOrderID =
                           SalesOrderDetail.SalesOrderID;
```

you get the following error:

```
Msg 515, Level 16, State 2, Line 125
Cannot insert the value NULL into column 'from_obj_id_75C28A838F1D4D618BB
8C1957919208E', table 'AdventureWorksLT2019.SalesGraph.Purchased'; column
does not allow nulls. INSERT fails.
```

The first time you do this might be a little bit confusing. It just means it tried to insert the two values and the object name provided did not reference an existing node table.

It has to be a node table, too; just any table will not work, which you can see if you execute the following statement that references the source relational table instead of the graph objects:

```
SELECT OBJECT_ID('SalesLT.Customer'),
       NODE_ID_FROM_PARTS(OBJECT_ID('SalesLT.Customer'), 1)
```

You will see that the NODE_ID_FROM_PARTS call returns NULL.

Heterogenous Queries

So far in the book, I have kept the pattern of usage for the designs to be one many-to-many relationship between just two nodes. Either the table was the same (Person-Follows-> Person) or different (Person-ProgramsWith->ProgrammingLanguage) but it was always one node to one node through a single edge. In this section, I want to highlight the ability to navigate multiple relationships through one edge, or even how you can traverse relationships through multiple edges.

As an example, you are going to add another set of nodes to the sample graph in the TestGraph database called Location. Then you will create edge values in the Follows edge. (Not that this makes logical sense, which is part of the point later in the example). See Figure 4-2.

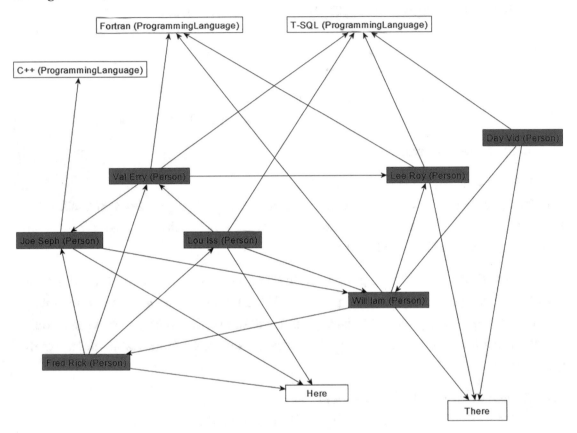

Figure 4-2. *Adding a new Location node type to the sample diagram*

Here is the DDL to create and DML to load this new table:

```
CREATE TABLE Network.Location
(
    LocationId INT NOT NULL IDENTITY,
    Name NVARCHAR(20) NOT NULL
        CONSTRAINT AKLocation UNIQUE
) AS NODE;

INSERT INTO Network.Location(    Name)
VALUES ('Here'),('There');
```

Now you associate the new rows with the items as shown on the diagram:

```
WITH Here
AS (SELECT Person.$node_id AS node_id
    FROM Network.Person
    WHERE Person.Name IN ( 'Fred Rick', 'Lou Iss', 'Joe Seph' ))

INSERT INTO Network.Follows
(  $from_id, $to_id, Value)
SELECT Here.node_id,
       Location.$node_id,
        1
FROM Here
    CROSS JOIN Network.Location
WHERE Location.Name = 'Here';

WITH There
AS (SELECT Person.$node_id AS node_id
    FROM Network.Person
    WHERE Person.Name IN ( 'Saa Lee', 'Lee Roy', 'Day Vid' ))

INSERT INTO Network.Follows
(  $from_id, $to_id, Value)
SELECT There.node_id,
       Location.$node_id,
        1
FROM There
    CROSS JOIN Network.Location
WHERE Location.Name = 'There';
```

Now you can see the rows you created like this:

```
SELECT Person.Name, Location.Name
FROM    Network.Person, Network.Follows, Network.Location
WHERE   Match(Person-(Follows)->Location);
```

This returns

Name	Name
Fred Rick	Here
Lou Iss	Here
Joe Seph	Here
Lee Roy	There
Saa Lee	There
Day Vid	There

So now you have two different kinds of nodes connected through the Network.
Follows edge. If you want to view them together, you can use a CTE or derived table to
union the object's data together. You don't have to include any of the graph structure
columns unless you want to output them. They are there because the object is a specific
type of object. In the following query, you see the locations and people that Lou Iss is
connected to through the Network.Follows edge:

```
SELECT Person.Name,
       Nodes.ObjectName,
       Nodes.Name
FROM Network.Person,
    Network.Follows,
(
    SELECT 'Location' AS ObjectName,
           Location.Name
    FROM Network.Location
    UNION ALL
    SELECT 'Person',
           Name
    FROM Network.Person
) AS Nodes
WHERE MATCH(Person-(Follows)->Nodes)
        AND Person.Name = 'Lou Iss';
```

This returns

Name	ObjectName	Name
Lou Iss	Person	Saa Lee
Lou Iss	Person	Val Erry
Lou Iss	Location	Here

Note that one of the main limitations of working with non-specific data in SQL Server shows itself here. Once you fetch the rows into a tabular data stream (TDS), they go back to being strongly typed and shaped relational tables. And since the method we are discussing requires a derived table, CTE, or view object, you need to shape the different sets of data to all be the same. This is a big limitation of this method in that you can't easily return something like the following without including all the columns in the UNION ALL, which gets tedious:

Name	ObjectName	Name	LocationDetails	PersonDetails
Lou Iss	Person	Saa Lee		Values
Lou Iss	Person	Val Erry		Values
Lou Iss	Location	Here		Values

Despite this limitation, it can be very useful for finding the relationship that one item has to the many other things it might be linked to.

For example, thinking of the Network schema as if it was a customer relationship management (CRM) system, how could you see everything that a customer is connected to, such as their preferences, the products they are interested in, locations, or stores they have shopped at? The output likely shows the user human-readable values (like Name or Label in my examples) and then a link to display more specific details.

For example,

```
SELECT OtherThing.ObjectType, OtherThing.Name,MoreDetailLink
FROM   Network.Person,
          --the graph columns are exposed automatically, and no
          --columns do you need, so just returning nothing
          --though this is clearly not a subquery about nothing
       (SELECT 1 AS nothing
        FROM Network.Follows
```

```
        UNION ALL
        SELECT 1
        FROM Network.ProgramsWith) as LinksTo,

    --this derived table is all things that someone can be
    --linked to
    (SELECT 'Person' as ObjectType, Name,
            CONCAT('https://getPerson/',PersonId)
                                        AS MoreDetailLink
      FROM Network.Person
      UNION ALL
      SELECT 'ProgrammingLanguage', ProgrammingLanguage.Name,
              CONCAT('https://getProgramming/',
                  ProgrammingLanguage.Name) AS MoreDetailLink
      FROM Network.ProgrammingLanguage
      UNION ALL
      SELECT 'Location',
              Location.Name,
            CONCAT('https://mapLocation/',LocationId)
                                        AS MoreDetailLink
      FROM Network.Location) AS OtherThing
WHERE  MATCH(Person-(LinksTo)->OtherThing)
  AND Person.Name = 'Lou Iss';
```

This code uses both edge objects and all three nodes you have defined so far to do all the relationships from the Lou Iss node.

```
ObjectType          Name         MoreDetailLink
------------------- ------------ --------------------------------
Person              Saa Lee      https://getPerson/5
Person              Val Erry     https://getPerson/3
Location            Here         https://mapLocation/1
ProgrammingLanguage T-SQL        https://getProgramming/T-SQL
```

If this is something you do regularly, you will most likely want to make this into view objects that you can reuse because the code is kind of messy. In the next block of code, translate the previous query with derived tables into a set of reusable view objects:

```
CREATE VIEW Network.LinksTo
AS
  SELECT 1 AS nothing FROM network.Follows
  UNION ALL
  SELECT 1 AS nothing FROM network.ProgramsWith;
GO

CREATE VIEW Network.Anything
as
  SELECT 'Person' as ObjectType,
          Person.Name,
           CONCAT('https://getPerson/',PersonId)
                                          AS MoreDetailLink
  FROM Network.Person
  UNION ALL
  SELECT 'ProgrammingLanguage',
          ProgrammingLanguage.Name,
          CONCAT('https://getProgramming/',
                      ProgrammingLanguage.Name) AS MoreDetailLink

  FROM     Network.ProgrammingLanguage
  UNION ALL
  SELECT 'Location',
         Location.Name,
         CONCAT('https://mapLocation/',LocationId)
                                            AS MoreDetailLink

  FROM     Network.Location;
```

Now the previous query can be written like this:

```
SELECT AnyThing.ObjectType, AnyThing.Name,
       Anything.MoreDetailLink
FROM    Network.Person, Network.LinksTo, Network.Anything
WHERE   MATCH(Person-(LinksTo)->AnyThing)
  AND Person.Name = 'Lou Iss';
```

What is interesting, though, is what happens if you add ,* to the SELECT clause. This should return all the columns, right? And since you were clearly able to join on the graph key values through the MATCH expression, you expect to see the values, right?

Turns out not. The only graph details you get are the $node_id from the Network. Person object. When your objects are encapsulated into derived tables or view objects, you only get access to the columns you output, even though the columns are in fact available for graph queries using MATCH.

The graph identifiers may not even be exposed in the same manner in all uses like this. For example,

```
SELECT Person.Name, Nodes.ObjectName, Nodes.Name,
       Nodes.$node_id
FROM   Network.Person, Network.Follows,
       (SELECT 'Location' as ObjectName, Name, $node_id
          FROM   Network.Person) as Nodes
WHERE MATCH(Person-(Follows)->Nodes)
  AND Person.Name = 'Lou Iss';
```

will throw this error:

```
Msg 207, Level 16, State 1, Line 243
Invalid column name '$node_id'.
```

even though it is clearly being used in the MATCH expression. If you want the graph identifier values to be part of the output, you must name them and use the name:

```
SELECT Nodes.ObjectName, Nodes.Name,
           Nodes.NodeId
FROM   Network.Person, Network.Follows,
       (SELECT 'Location' AS ObjectName, Name,
                     $node_id AS NodeId
          FROM   Network.Person) AS Nodes
WHERE MATCH(Person-(Follows)->Nodes)
 AND Person.Name = 'Lou Iss';
```

This returns

```
ObjectName Name        NodeId
---------- ----------  -------------------------------------------
Location   Saa Lee     {"type":"node","schema":"Network","tab...
Location   Val Erry    {"type":"node","schema":"Network","tab...
```

Likewise, you need to include the implementation columns you need in your view definition if you need them for some reason.

Integrity Constraints and Indexes

One of my favorite things to say about building a typical relational database system is that *the first, last, and only thing that truly matters is that your data is correct*. Fast and wrong is worse than slow and right. In this section, you will learn some of the ways that you can ensure correct data. Of course, correct and fast is clearly desirable, so you will also see some of the indexes that you need to add to your objects for performance enhancements.

Edge Constraint

So far in Chapters 3 and 4, I have been careful with the data we have put into the edge tables. As any software developer knows, flexibility is a pro and a con. Sometimes as a designer you think that flexibility will be used for good only, but then data starts creeping in that is meaningless and starts to have ill effects on the user experience (and confidence).

In my example tables, the design didn't consider the concept that someone could try to put illogical data into the tables. For example, right now it is perfectly acceptable to the structures to say that Lou Iss-ProgramsWith-> Here or T-SQL-ProgramsWith->C++. Both are illogical statements.

The classic integrity constraints you should know already (foreign key, check, unique, primary key, default) all generally work with graph tables just like they do with normal relational tables. (There are limitations like not using graph key values in check constraints.) However, because an edge table can have more than one source of data for the $from_id and $end_id, there needed to be a new type of constraint. It's called the **edge constraint**.

The edge constraint limits what data can be put into an edge by node objects, both to and from. For example, when you built the relationship for the homogenous section of this chapter, you created data, effectively implementing the relationship `Person->Follows->Location`. Since you are defining where a person is located, this relationship makes no sense semantically, so you want to change that to have its own edge: `LivesAt`, or `Person-LivesAt->Location`. After you make this change, you are going to make sure that you cannot say that a person lives at a programming language or follows a location. Along the way of moving the rows to this new edge, you can see the things that can happen with an edge object and how to constrain the data to a proper set.

You can define multiple paths through the data in a single edge constraint. As an initial example, let's add a constraint to the `Network.Follows` edge that will accept the data that is currently in the table to show how to do multiple tables. For the `Network.Follows` edge, you are going to allow `Network.Person` to `Network.Person` and then the `Network.Person` to `Network.Location` (which you will work to remove):

```
ALTER TABLE Network.Follows
ADD CONSTRAINT EC_Follows CONNECTION
     (Network.Person TO Network.Location,
       Network.Person TO Network.Person) ON DELETE NO ACTION;
```

The `NO ACTION` setting on the `DELETE` operation means you cannot delete a related node in either connected table without deleting all edges that are connected. If you use `CASCADE` instead of `NO ACTION`, a delete of a node in either table would cause the edge row to be removed. (I won't demonstrate it, but you could easily construct an after-trigger object that could delete an edge row only when the from member node (or to, if that is your requirement) was deleted and fail for the other item if you need very customized relationships.)

One of the stranger things about edge constraints is that while you can have more than one at a time, their conditions are ANDed together. So, you can't add conditions with a new edge constraint without including any data that is currently in the edge. And the error message you get when you try will have you scratching your head the first time you encounter it.

For example, if you add this additional constraint along with the `EC_Follows` constraint added earlier

```
ALTER TABLE Network.Follows
  ADD CONSTRAINT EC_Follows2 CONNECTION
```

```
(Network.Person TO Network.ProgrammingLanguage)
    ON DELETE NO ACTION;
```

this will return the following error message. Instinctively, this error message doesn't feel true.

```
Msg 547, Level 16, State 0, Line 383
The ALTER TABLE statement conflicted with the EDGE constraint "EC_
Follows2". The conflict occurred in database "TestGraph", table "Network.
Follows".
```

So, usually you need to include all the relationships from the previous constraint in the new one (which is useful when you need to make a change to a live table). In this demonstration, you are going to delete the EC_Follows constraint because you have data to clean up:

```
ALTER TABLE Network.Follows DROP EC_Follows;
```

Now let's delete one of the location rows (not needed for your ultimate goal, but you are doing it here to see what happens without a constraint):

```
DELETE Network.Location
WHERE Location.NAME = 'Here';
```

Looking at the data in the edge, something is odd now. Check to make sure you have deleted the row, and look at the $node_id value:

```
SELECT Location.Name,$node_id
FROM Network.Location;
```

There is only the one location (I shorted the $node_id on the left-hand side so you could see the id, which has a value of 1):

```
Name       $node_id_706A69FC56E046AF955F94567D088822
---------- ----------------------------------------------------
There.     ...schema":"Network","table":"Location","id":1}
```

If you look at the following query

```
SELECT Follows.$to_id,COUNT(*)
FROM Network.Follows
WHERE Follows.$to_id LIKE '%location%'
GROUP BY Follows.$to_id;
```

instinctively you probably think that you could only have rows from the Location table that have an id value of 1, because that is the only actual id value that remains.

```
$to_id_EF1AB6E3676C45CDABD558C4D40746B4
------------------------------------------------------------- -
{"type":"node","schema":"Network","table":"Location","id":0}  3
{"type":"node","schema":"Network","table":"Location","id":1}  3
```

You will see two rows (with 3 for the second column of both, most likely if you haven't added your own data) … since you haven't protected against duplicates yet, you might have done what I did and added extras.

You can find the offending row using a bit messier query, assuming you know the table you expect the issue to be from. If you have a bunch of tables, it can be quite a challenge! (So, use constraints to start and never have these issues!)

```
SELECT DISTINCT OBJECT_SCHEMA_NAME(OBJECT_ID_FROM_NODE_ID(Follows.$to_id)),
      OBJECT_NAME(OBJECT_ID_FROM_NODE_ID(Follows.$to_id)),
      Follows.$to_id
FROM Network.Follows
WHERE Follows.$to_id NOT IN --check to see values that don't
                          --exist in the node tables
    (
        SELECT Person.$node_id
        FROM Network.Person
        UNION ALL
        SELECT ProgrammingLanguage.$node_id
        FROM Network.ProgrammingLanguage
        UNION ALL
        SELECT $node_id
        FROM Network.Location
    );
```

This will tell you the object where the key values come from and the key value so you can delete the edge rows where you have an issue, like this one:

```
DELETE Network.Follows
WHERE  Follows.$to_id = '{"type":"node","schema":"Network","table":"Location",
"id":0}';
```

Now let's put the edge constraint back on with the two tables, but this time with CASCADE:

```
ALTER TABLE Network.Follows
ADD CONSTRAINT EC_Follows CONNECTION
   (Network.Person TO Network.Location,
    Network.Person TO Network.Person)
       ON DELETE CASCADE;
```

Using the following query, you will see the number of rows from each table that is referenced in the Network.Follows edge:

```
SELECT
      OBJECT_SCHEMA_NAME(OBJECT_ID_FROM_NODE_ID(Follows.$to_id)),
      OBJECT_NAME(OBJECT_ID_FROM_NODE_ID(Follows.$to_id)),
      COUNT(*)
FROM Network.Follows
GROUP BY OBJECT_SCHEMA_NAME(OBJECT_ID_FROM_NODE_ID(Follows.$to_id)),
         OBJECT_NAME(OBJECT_ID_FROM_NODE_ID(Follows.$to_id));
```

In my version of the table, I have 11 references to Network.Person and 3 to Network.Location. Now just delete the Network.Location rows and the rows will be gone from the edge:

```
DELETE FROM Network.Location;
```

The output shows 1 row affected, but if you run the previous SELECT statement again, in my database there are 10 Network.Person rows in the Network.Follows table. So now you can change the constraint:

```
ALTER TABLE Network.Follows
ADD CONSTRAINT EC_Follows CONNECTION
   (Network.Person TO Network.Person)
       ON DELETE CASCADE;
```

I set it to NO ACTION because I typically prefer to delete the rows manually rather than have them just automatically go away. Many database coding mistakes have been exacerbated by using CASCADE functionality!

Next, create a new edge for the Network.Person to Network.Location relationship with an edge constraint to prevent any data other than associating a person to a location:

```
CREATE TABLE Network.LivesAt
(
    CONSTRAINT EC_LivesAt CONNECTION
            (Network.Person TO Network.Location)
) AS EDGE;

INSERT INTO Network.Location
(
    NAME
)
VALUES
('Here'),
('There');
```

Finally, add back the data to restore the data to match the model in Figure 4-2:

```
WITH Here
AS (SELECT Person.$node_id AS node_id
    FROM Network.Person
    WHERE Person.NAME IN ( 'Fred Rick', 'Lou Iss', 'Joe Seph' ))
INSERT INTO Network.LivesAt
(
    $from_id,
    $to_id
)
SELECT Here.node_id,
       Location.$node_id
FROM Here
    CROSS JOIN Network.Location
WHERE Location.NAME = 'Here';

WITH Here
AS (SELECT Person.$node_id AS node_id
    FROM Network.Person
    WHERE Person.NAME IN ('Saa Lee', 'Lee Roy', 'Day Vid' ))
```

```
INSERT INTO Network.LivesAt
(
    $from_id,
    $to_id
)
SELECT Here.node_id,
      Location.$node_id
FROM Here
    CROSS JOIN Network.Location
WHERE Location.NAME = 'There';
```

Now the data matches the diagram.

Uniqueness Constraints (and Indexes)

As you probably know, one of the more painful parts of working with a set of data is when you have undesired duplicated data. This is no different when working with graph structures; in fact, because the actual columns are encapsulated away from you **most** of the time, it can be worse. I stress **most** because the physical implementation details are not completely hidden from you and show up in some places you might not expect.

As an example, you are going to insert rows that are identical to the second set of rows in the previous section (by using the exact same SQL statement):

```
WITH Here
AS (SELECT Person.$node_id AS node_id
    FROM Network.Person
    WHERE Person.NAME IN ( 'Saa Lee', 'Lee Roy', 'Day Vid' ))
INSERT INTO Network.LivesAt
(
    $from_id,
    $to_id
)
SELECT Here.node_id,
      Location.$node_id
FROM Here
    CROSS JOIN Network.Location
WHERE Location.NAME = 'There';
```

Note that now you have duplicated data:

```
SELECT Person.Name,
       Location.Name
FROM Network.Person,
     Network.LivesAt,
     Network.Location
WHERE MATCH(Person-(LivesAt)->Location)
          AND Location.NAME = 'There'
ORDER BY Person.Name;
```

The output of this query is

NAME	NAME
Day Vid	There
Day Vid	There
Lee Roy	There
Lee Roy	There
Saa Lee	There
Saa Lee	There

To prevent this, you can use unique constraints that reference the pseudocolumns. For example, after deleting the rows for the duplicated There location values

```
DELETE LivesAt
FROM Network.Person,Network.LivesAt,Network.Location
WHERE MATCH(Person-(LivesAt)->Location)
          AND Location.NAME = 'There';
```

now create the following uniqueness constraint on the $from_id and $to_id. This prevents the user from creating the same relationship over and over, something that is generally not desirable.

```
ALTER TABLE Network.LivesAt
  ADD CONSTRAINT AKLivesAt_FromIdToId UNIQUE ($from_id, $to_id);
```

Unique constraints are implemented in SQL Server as indexes, and this index is going to be valuable in breadth-first algorithms anyhow. Now try the insert of rows with the location of There a couple of times, repeatedly.

On the second run, you get an error message with values like the following:

```
Msg 2627, Level 14, State 1, Line 454 Violation of UNIQUE KEY constraint
'AKLivesAt_FromIdToId'. Cannot insert duplicate key in object 'Network.
LivesAt'. The duplicate key value is (581577110, 3, 933578364, 3).
```

What the heck are those numbers in the error message? They are the keys in the underlying graph objects. While the values you typically see look like a long piece of JSON in an nvarchar(1000) value, actually the implementation is translating all of that into integer values.

The key values translate to the object_id of the source table and graph the internal id. To translate these values, implement the following tool function to look up the values:

```
IF SCHEMA_ID('Tools') IS NULL
  EXEC ('CREATE SCHEMA Tools')
GO
CREATE OR ALTER PROCEDURE Tools.GraphDB$LookupItem
    @ObjectId int,
    @Id int
AS
BEGIN
    SET NOCOUNT ON;
    DECLARE @SchemaName sysname =
        OBJECT_SCHEMA_NAME(@ObjectId),
        @TableName sysname = OBJECT_NAME(@ObjectId),
        @SQLStatement nvarchar(MAX)
    SET @SQLStatement = CONCAT('SELECT * FROM ',
        QUOTENAME(@SchemaName),'.',QUOTENAME(@TableName),
        WHERE GRAPH_ID_FROM_NODE_ID($node_id)  = ',@Id)

    EXECUTE (@SQLStatement)
END;
```

Now you can look up the items easily:

```
EXEC Tools.GraphDB$LookupItem 581577110, 3;
EXEC Tools.GraphDB$LookupItem 933578364, 3;
```

This returns the row that contains the data that was duplicated (this may not exist if you inserted both rows in the same transaction and rolled back).

Beyond uniqueness constraints (which you can put on one or both of the _id columns, and you can also include other columns in your edge table), you may want to add indexes to your graph edges to help performance.

There are some indexes already on your object, for example on the Network.LivesAt edge table you just created. Using the sys.indexes catalog view, you can see what is on the object by default:

```
SELECT indexes.name,
       indexes.type_desc
FROM sys.indexes
WHERE indexes.OBJECT_ID = OBJECT_ID('Network.LivesAt');
```

Three rows are returned. One indicates your object is heap. Another is for the AKLivesAt_FromIdToId unique constraint. And then there is an index that will look something like GRAPH_UNIQUE_INDEX_AD2E365DF5144A62BEBC7C7260258E2A. This is an index that is on the internal graph columns, but there is no clustered index. You can actually change the AK index that references the internal columns to be clustered, or even make it a PRIMARY KEY constraint (that is clustered by default):

```
ALTER TABLE Network.LivesAt
  DROP CONSTRAINT AKLivesAt_FromIdToId;

ALTER TABLE Network.LivesAt
  ADD CONSTRAINT AKLivesAt_FromIdToId  UNIQUE CLUSTERED
      ($from_id, $to_id);
```

Take a look at the query of sys.indexes again. Now it is clustered. This can be very helpful for certain types of workloads that mostly fetch data by the $from_id value (or $to_id value, depending on how you structure the index to meet your normal pattern of usage) which you know to be two columns from the duplicate key error. You can see that in the sys.index_columns catalog view:

```
SELECT indexes.name,
       indexes.type_desc,
       index_columns.key_ordinal,
       columns.name
FROM sys.index_columns
    JOIN sys.indexes
        ON indexes.object_id = index_columns.object_id
            AND indexes.index_id = index_columns.index_id
    JOIN sys.columns
        ON indexes.object_id = columns.object_id
            AND columns.column_id = index_columns.column_id
WHERE indexes.object_id = OBJECT_ID('Network.LivesAt');
```

Additional Constraints

Depending on what your requirements are for your graph, you may need to add more constraints to your data. Unfortunately, you are not allowed to use a CHECK constraint object on the pseudocolumns.

One of the most frequent needs is to disallow self-relationships. Having a node follow itself makes no semantic sense in most models. My first inclination was to just create a constraint:

```
ALTER TABLE Network.Follows
    ADD CONSTRAINT CHKFollows_NoSelfReference
        CHECK ($to_id <> $from_id);
```

But this failed, hard:

```
Msg 13918, Level 16, State 1, Line 656
Adding constraint to column '$from_id' of a node or edge table is not allowed.
```

Trying to use the full column name without square brackets treats the column names as different pseudocolumns:

```
ALTER TABLE Network.Follows
    ADD CONSTRAINT CHKFollows_NoSelfReference CHECK
        ($from_id_86757ACD89174977A9D8380F484416AE <>
            $to_id_EF1AB6E3676C45CDABD558C4D40746B4)
```

This returns

```
Msg 126, Level 15, State 2, Line 663
Invalid pseudocolumn "$from_id_86757ACD89174977A9D8380F484416AE".
```

Putting square brackets around the column names (since that is how they show up in sys.columns)

```
ALTER TABLE Network.Follows
    ADD CONSTRAINT CHKFollows_NoSelfReference CHECK
    ([$from_id_86757ACD89174977A9D8380F484416AE] <>
    [$to_id_EF1AB6E3676C45CDABD558C4D40746B4])
```

just takes you back to the first error message (and you really don't want to reference these column names in code anyhow, because even recreating the table on the same server will give you different names, much less the pain of managing code on multiple environments):

```
Msg 13918, Level 16, State 1, Line 662
Adding constraint to column '$from_id' of a node or edge table is not
allowed.
```

So, if you want to constrain data in your edge tables as it pertains to the pseudocolumns, you need to use a trigger. Before building that trigger, let's insert a row where $from_id and $to_id are the same:

```
INSERT INTO Network.Follows
(
    $from_id,
    $to_id,
    Value
)
SELECT (SELECT Person.$node_id FROM Network.Person WHERE Person.FirstName =
'Fred' AND Person.LastName = 'Rick'),

        (SELECT Person.$node_id FROM Network.Person WHERE Person.FirstName =
        'Fred' AND Person.LastName = 'Rick'),
        1
```

As an aside, a row like this where the person row is related to the same person row is actually the only possible way for the following query to return data:

```
SELECT Person.Name
FROM.    Network.Person, Network.Follows
WHERE MATCH(Person-(Follows)->Person);
```

Reusing an edge isn't allowed, but reusing a node is. However, when you reuse a node, it is exactly the same set of data filtered by itself. So, the MATCH expression ends up just being logically translated to

```
WHERE Person.$node_id = Follows.$from_id
  AND Person.$node_id = Follows.$to_id
```

Since the $node_id is not an array (you are, of course, still in a relational database) there could never be rows returned. The only row that could be returned is one where Fred Follows Fred.

So, you have to do it the hard way, by using an after trigger object. Note that in the first section of this chapter, you used an INSTEAD OF trigger on a view object. INSTEAD OF triggers are typically used to alter DML operations. But now you just want to check to see if things are correct after the operation has completed.

To code this trigger, you are going to use a slightly modified trigger template from my *Database Design* book (removing the error logging capabilities) because error handling from a trigger is better if you control how errors are raised and dealt with.

Note   This trigger template can be found here: `https://github.com/drsqlgithub/dbdesignbook6/tree/master/Appendix%20B`.

```
CREATE TRIGGER Network.Follows$InsertUpdateTrigger
ON Network.Follows
AFTER INSERT,UPDATE AS --make 2 triggers if you need
                       --them to do anything different
BEGIN
    SET NOCOUNT ON; --to avoid the rowcount messages
    SET ROWCOUNT 0; --in case the client has modified the rowcount

    DECLARE @msg varchar(2000), --used to hold the error message
```

```
        @rowsAffected int = (SELECT COUNT(*) FROM inserted);

--no need to continue on if no rows affected
IF @rowsAffected = 0 RETURN;

BEGIN TRY
        --[validation section]
        IF EXISTS (SELECT *
                    FROM Inserted
                    WHERE $from_id = $to_id)
          BEGIN
                SET @msg = '$from_id must not equal' +
                            ' $to_id when modifying edge';
                THROW 50000, @msg, 1;
          END;
        --[modification section]
END TRY
BEGIN CATCH
    IF @@trancount > 0
        ROLLBACK TRANSACTION;

    THROW; --will halt the batch or be caught
            --by the caller's catch block
            --with the transaction aborted.
    END CATCH;
END;
```

The duplicate row can be removed by executing the following statement:

```
DELETE
FROM    Network.Follows
WHERE   Follows.$from_id = Follows.$to_id;
```

Now trying to do the following insert:

```
INSERT INTO Network.Follows
(
    $from_id,
    $to_id,
```

```
    Value
)
SELECT (SELECT Person.$node_id FROM Network.Person
        WHERE Person.FirstName = 'Fred'
          AND Person.LastName = 'Rick'),
        (SELECT Person.$node_id FROM Network.Person
         WHERE Person.FirstName = 'Fred'
           AND Person.LastName = 'Rick'),
        1;
```

You get this as a return:

```
Msg 50000, Level 16, State 1, Procedure
Follows$InsertUpdateTrigger, Line 21
$from_id must not equal $to_id when modifying edge
```

One thing to note is that the $from_id and $to_id are exposed in the trigger with the inserted and deleted objects, so you can do pretty much anything you want with that JSON for validating the data.

Metadata Roundup

To end the introductory segment of the book, I want to show/review some of the metadata you can use to find the details of your graph objects.

List Graph Objects in the Database

```
SELECT OBJECT_SCHEMA_NAME(tables.object_id) AS schema_name,
       tables.name,
       CASE
           WHEN tables.is_node = 1 THEN
               'Node'
           WHEN tables.is_edge = 1 THEN
               'Edge'
           ELSE
               'Bad code!'
```

```
        END as object_type
FROM sys.tables
WHERE tables.is_node = 1
      OR tables.is_edge = 1
ORDER BY schema_name, tables.name;
```

The output of this query shows you the objects you worked with in the main example in the last two chapters.

Types of Graph Columns

Sometimes you need to see the physical column names for your graph db objects. The following two queries show the columns from a node and an edge:

```
SELECT columns.name,
       columns.column_id,
       CASE
           WHEN columns.name LIKE '$%' THEN
               1
           ELSE
               0
       END AS has_pseudocolumn,
       columns.graph_type_desc
FROM sys.COLUMNS
WHERE OBJECT_ID('Network.Person') = COLUMNS.OBJECT_ID
      AND columns.graph_type_desc IS NOT NULL;

SELECT columns.name,
       columns.column_id,
       CASE
           WHEN columns.name LIKE '$%' THEN
               1
           ELSE
               0
       END AS has_pseudocolumn,
       columns.graph_type_desc
FROM sys.columns
```

```
WHERE OBJECT_ID('Network.Follows') = COLUMNS.OBJECT_ID
    AND columns.graph_type_desc IS NOT NULL;
```

Executing these queries, you get the following:

NAME	column_id	has_pseudocolumn	graph_type_desc
graph_id_F8B...	1	0	GRAPH_ID
$node_id_C01...	2	1	GRAPH_ID_COMPUTED

NAME	column_id	has_pseudocolumn	graph_type_desc
graph_id_240...	1	0	GRAPH_ID
$edge_id_EF2...	2	1	GRAPH_ID_COMPUTED
from_obj_iA6...	3	0	GRAPH_FROM_OBJ_ID
from_id_4E69...	4	0	GRAPH_FROM_ID
$from_id_857...	5	1	GRAPH_FROM_ID_COMPUTED
to_obj_id_08...	6	0	GRAPH_TO_OBJ_ID
to_id_C0A723...	7	0	GRAPH_TO_ID
$to_id_EF16E...	8	1	GRAPH_TO_ID_COMPUTED

The column name has been greatly shrunken (for example, the first query's $node_dc59... column is actually $node_id_C580185613BB42EF81F4A68F6FA539DC). But the interesting parts here are that you can see there is a computed column that corresponds to the $from_id, but there are two columns for each $node_id value. Plus, there is a GRAPH_ID column that each table has but you don't have access to.

Currently the value of this will be the same for all objects. You only have one graph structure per database (much like you can only have one in-memory structure per database as well).

Tools for Fetching Graph Information

I won't even pretend I can put the contents of this next query into the text of this chapter, but the basic idea is to show you all of the functions and how you pull apart the graph internal values if you need to do so from time to time:

```
SELECT OBJECT_ID_FROM_EDGE_ID(Follows.$edge_id) AS
                                            FollowsObjectId,
       GRAPH_ID_FROM_EDGE_ID(Follows.$edge_id) AS FollowsEdgeId,
       OBJECT_ID_FROM_NODE_ID(Follows.$from_id) AS FromObjectId,
       OBJECT_SCHEMA_NAME(OBJECT_ID_FROM_NODE_ID
                  (Follows.$from_id)) AS FromObjectSchemaName,
       OBJECT_NAME(OBJECT_ID_FROM_NODE_ID(Follows.$from_id))
                                              AS FromObjectName,
       GRAPH_ID_FROM_NODE_ID(Follows.$from_id) AS FromGraphId,
       OBJECT_ID_FROM_NODE_ID(Follows.$to_id) AS ToObjectId,
       GRAPH_ID_FROM_NODE_ID(Follows.$to_id) AS ToGraphId,
       OBJECT_SCHEMA_NAME(OBJECT_ID_FROM_NODE_ID(Follows.$to_id))
                                           AS ToObjectSchemaName,
       OBJECT_NAME(OBJECT_ID_FROM_NODE_ID(Follows.$from_id))
                                            AS ToObjectName
FROM Network.Follows;
```

You can look at a row using the following function if you happen to have the object_
id and the graph id value. You just randomly picked out a row from the output, but often
you have these values, as I showed earlier in the error message:

```
SELECT Person.$node_id,
       Person.PersonId,
       Person.FirstName,
       Person.LastName,
       Person.NAME,
       Person.Value
FROM Network.Person
WHERE Person.$node_id = NODE_ID_FROM_PARTS(581577110, 5);
```

Summary

In this chapter, you finished out the introductory topics, with the goal of learning most of
the syntax and techniques that you will be using in the rest of the book.

You learned a few techniques for loading data into graph tables easier than coding the look-up for the $node_id values. The first was building a data interface that lets you insert data into a table in a manner that feels like a normal table by letting you ignore the graph columns while still getting the value of the graph data structures. The second was pushing data directly into the graph values from other existing data.

Then you covered heterogenous queries, where you can treat multiple edges and nodes as one in certain situations (for example, a customer database where you want to see everything you know about the customer in one straightforward query.) The biggest downside for doing this with SQL Server objects is that you are still bound by the concepts of a relational database's rows and column rigidness. So, you must forge the various tables into something that has the same row/column shape for such queries, but it is quite useful once you do.

From there you moved onto protecting your data with integrity constraints include edge and uniqueness constraints, plus triggers for cases where you can't use declarative constraints. I briefly mention indexes for performance, but that is something that will be situationally based.

Finally, you learned some of the metadata you can find in SQL Server and how you can use it for multiple reasons.

This ends the discussion of how you do basic graph operations. In the following chapters, you will build example databases to see how create and optimize real solutions.

CHAPTER 5

Tree Data Structures

A tree is one of the more typical graph structures you will implement using a SQL Server database. As covered in Chapter 1, a tree is a directed acyclic graph (DAG) where every node can only have one parent relationship. In other worlds, the node can only participate as the to in zero or one relationship. In Chapter 7, you will implement a general DAG structure, but it will share some similarity to trees when utilizing the data structures.

There are two main reasons tree structures are common. First, they are data structures that meet a need that almost every company has: the ability to roll up activity (sales, for example) from the people who do the work to the people who manage or coordinate that work and then to the regions where that work is performed. For example, a company like Microsoft needs to know its total income for the year. This information must also be broken down into business units, individual products, individual sales groups for that product, and so on. Microsoft probably also has a tree structure that breaks data down into regions, product lines, and colors as well. The tree structure inherently prohibits duplication, so it is perfect for rolling up monetary attribution.

Second, due to the relatively fixed shape of a tree, implementing a tree has been reasonable for years. It is also possible to performance-tune tree queries on even a very large dataset (something that is less reasonable on a cyclic graph structure that can grow in many different directions at once).

My first introduction to the topic was well over 20 years ago when I went to a workshop taught by Dr. David Rozenshtein. He wrote one of the most influential books of my career (*The Essence of SQL*) and was in the middle of writing a book on trees that he gave us after the workshop. I don't think he actually finished that book (*Tree and Graph Processing in SQL*) as even today it is listed in Amazon as "Preview Edition." Sadly, as this was three job changes, 25 years, and five houses ago, I don't have these books anymore, but some of the techniques taught in that class are still in use today.

That class started a longstanding fascination with tree structures and the many ways to implement them. I will discuss more of this in Chapter 6 when I introduce an additional method to implement a graph for high performance access.

© Louis Davidson 2023
L. Davidson, *Practical Graph Structures in SQL Server and Azure SQL*,
https://doi.org/10.1007/978-1-4842-9459-8_5

In this chapter, I provide the base code you need to implement a working tree structure using SQL Server's graph database structures. This includes all the code to create the objects, maintain the nodes and edges, and then create code that will be very common in most implementations (and in the next chapter, I use that code to put the structures through some tests.) The output of this chapter is a set of objects and data that implements the data structure introduced back in Chapter 2 and represented in Figure 5-1.

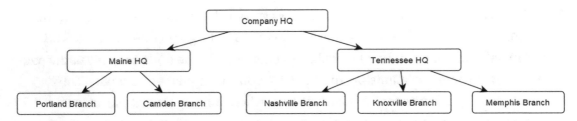

Figure 5-1. *Small set of data for demonstrating graph object*

I cover the basic techniques needed to manage this data structure in this chapter, such as adding, removing, and moving nodes and then querying the nodes to roll up activity from parent to child.

Creating the Data Structures

To get started, let's create a database, a schema, and the tables needed to hold the data. In the GitHub repo for the book for Chapter 5, there is a script with fillable parameters to create the database named 0000-Create The GraphDBTests Database.sql. It generated a large enough database to do all the examples in Chapter 6 as well. The database name is GraphDBTests.

Base Table Structures

To start this process, create a schema. The schema name represents the algorithm/ pattern for this specific example. In later examples where I vary the pattern for different methods of implementing a tree, I differentiate the sample code with schema names that represent those algorithms. This lets me build the same example structures and load scripts with the only difference being the name of the schema.

```
CREATE SCHEMA SqlGraph;
```

The Company node is a basic object with just name and surrogate key value columns. Consider this object to be analogous to your typical customer table in any database, only missing many of the other attributes you might want in your object when you are building your real databases. In some designs, you might have a relational Company table and join to the Company node table when you want to deal with it in comparison/position to other Company rows.

Both columns in the Company table have uniqueness constraints, and the surrogate integer key (CompanyId) is the clustering key (it is possible to cluster on the $node_id pseudocolumn, which may be useful if you have many columns you need to fetch by the $node_id). Unlike a simple adjacency list, which might contain a column named like "ParentCompanyId" to indicate the hierarchy, as you saw using SQL Graph objects in the previous chapters, the graph structures are in a separate table that is defined as an edge.

```
CREATE TABLE SqlGraph.Company
(
    CompanyId INT IDENTITY(1, 1)
        CONSTRAINT PKCompany PRIMARY KEY,
    Name VARCHAR(20) NOT NULL
        CONSTRAINT AKCompany_Name UNIQUE,
    RootNodeFlag bit
        CONSTRAINT DFLTCompany_RootNodeFlag DEFAULT(0)
) AS NODE;
```

The RootNodeFlag is very useful when processing the tree at times because it will give you a starting point that you don't have to calculate (or strictly know the name of the node in queries.) The default constraint will make it such that you only have to think about it in your DML when creating the one root node. To this, you add the following index to make sure that there is only one root node:

```
CREATE UNIQUE INDEX rootNode ON SqlGraph.Company (RootNodeFlag)
WHERE RootNodeFlag = 1;
```

There are no extra columns in this edge, but you might in a real table want to include at least the time when the row was created and maybe a time when the relationship was established. They might be the same time but likely should not be the same column since the relationship might have been established earlier than the row was created.

Even when data is coming in real time (for example, from a web interface) you might want data to go through some workflow before being inserted into your main database. Keeping this example simple will simply keep the example simple (duh!) so it basically covers the one aspect we care about... implementing a tree. When I compare other algorithms to this one, the most important thing is that we do the same things for the other objects.

Creating the edge for a tree (as it will for almost any directed acyclic graph) will all be links from a node to a node of the very same type, so I will include the edge constraint to make sure. Clearly, in a database like this, with only one node table, this is implied, but when you want to test performance and functionality, it is always best to make your structures follow as best design practices as possible.

```
CREATE TABLE SqlGraph.ReportsTo
(
    CONSTRAINT EC_ReportsTo$DefinesParentOf
        CONNECTION (SqlGraph.Company TO SqlGraph.Company)
                ON DELETE NO ACTION
)
AS EDGE;
```

Next, let's add a few indexes to support the types of queries you will be executing.

The first is a clustered index, and for this structure you will cluster the table on the $to_id value. This is because the most common (and expensive) queries will be fetching rows based on the $to_id. While you will not have to write your own breadth-first queries for trees, internally that is exactly what will occur, and the columns the $to_id represents is the lead in all of those queries. Make it a UNIQUE constraint because for this object to be a strict tree, each $to_id should only show up once in the structure.

Note that you could implement multiple tree structures in the same object by adding a name for the specific structures in the object and including it in the unique index. I won't do that as any specific example because the code is very much the same, except for filtering on the tree segment you are working with.

```
ALTER TABLE SqlGraph.ReportsTo
    ADD CONSTRAINT AKReportsTo UNIQUE CLUSTERED ($to_id);
```

The second index is actually on the `$from_id` column. When you do any queries for the parent of a node, this index will be useful.

```
CREATE INDEX FromId ON SqlGraph.ReportsTo($from_id);
```

There will be a few specific demonstrations of performance I will be using to compare algorithms, both of which mirror activity that you will likely need for many of your actual tree objects.

One of these is summing the activity of child objects. This is analogous to a company that has sales in multiple regions, and you need to see the sales for each region. Of course, as is typical, regions can have subregions and so on down to different locations. There is no requirement that the tree have any shape. One region could stand alone, and another could be broken down into hundreds of different subregions.

In the simple case, you will start with a very balanced tree, but you will see how to modify it to be unbalanced. In the next chapter, the tables will be populated with quite large sets of data randomly generated so they will not be perfectly balanced, simply to give the examples a bit more reality.

Demo Sales Structure

The following object is not actually part of the graph itself but is used to generate some Company sales data. You will use a straightforward algorithm to generate this data, so the same sales rows are always generated for the tester.

To do this, use a SEQUENCE object to give each customer an increasing amount of sales (though for sake of easy, the number of sales is set to 5). The SEQUENCE object makes the process a lot more straightforward than with an identity property on a column because you can put it in the stored procedure and if you want to use a different method, it is far easier to replace.

```
CREATE SEQUENCE SqlGraph.CompanyDataGenerator_SEQUENCE
AS INT
START WITH 1;
GO

CREATE TABLE SqlGraph.Sale
(
    SalesId int NOT NULL IDENTITY(1, 1)
            CONSTRAINT PKSale PRIMARY KEY,
```

```
TransactionNumber varchar(10) NOT NULL
            CONSTRAINT AKSale UNIQUE,
    Amount              numeric(12, 2) NOT NULL,
    CompanyId           int            NOT NULL
            CONSTRAINT FKSale$Ref$Company
                    REFERENCES SqlGraph.Company(CompanyId),
    INDEX XCompanyId (CompanyId, Amount)
);
```

The SqlGraph.Sale table is here for when you do aggregations to make the situation more "real." Note that the code uses a sequential number from the SEQUENCE object for the Amount multiplied by .25.

This is the stored procedure for creating the test sales data:

```
CREATE PROCEDURE SqlGraph.Sale$InsertTestData
    @Name       varchar(20),
        --Note that all procs use natural keys to make it easier
        --for you to work with manually.
        --If you are implementing this for a tool to manipulate,
        --use surrogate keys where possible
    @RowCount int = 5
        --you can vary the number of sales, if you want
AS
BEGIN
    SET NOCOUNT ON;

    WHILE @RowCount > 0
    BEGIN
        INSERT INTO SqlGraph.Sale(TransactionNumber, Amount,
                    CompanyId)
        --two NEXT VALUE FOR statements return the same value
        --in the same code.
        SELECT CAST(NEXT VALUE FOR
                    SqlGraph.CompanyDataGenerator_SEQUENCE
                AS varchar(10)),
            .25 * CAST(NEXT VALUE FOR
                    SqlGraph.CompanyDataGenerator_SEQUENCE
```

```
                        AS numeric(12, 2)),
                    --fetch the surrogate key
            (   SELECT Company.CompanyId
                FROM    SqlGraph.Company
                WHERE   Company.Name = @Name);

        SET @RowCount = @RowCount - 1;
    END;
END;
```

You will see the output of executing this code later in the chapter.

Essential Tree Maintenance Code

In this section, you will build a coded object to create new rows in the node table. This code is interesting for reuse if you are building a real system. Note that I have omitted some error handling for clarity of the demos, but I have tried to include transactions and TRY CATCH blocks in most code so the code is minimally acceptable for even production systems.

Some of the techniques you looked at in Chapter 4 (like including a trigger object to make processing more natural) will not be used in this chapter because this code is going to simulate the more real process of creating rows as the customer might do in real customer activity, one at a time. Tree structures are very often a part of an online transaction processing system (OLTP) system and the data could be modified while others are using the data.

One variation from "real code" is that in all the code presented, you use natural key values for the parameters, so the scripts don't have to care what the internal implementation is. If you are building a stored procedure interface for an application, you should generally use the primary key, but when building an interface you work with in an ad-hoc manner, natural keys that make sense to the user are far easier to deal with.

Note   Having your code access data by the clustering key is best, when possible, in your production-worthy code. It eliminates a read to the table that incurs an unnecessary bookmark lookup. For more information about performance tuning, I suggest referring to Grant Fritchey's *SQL Server 2022 Query Performance Tuning: Troubleshoot and Optimize Query Performance Sixth Edition.*

Code To Create New Nodes

Creating new nodes is an essential piece of code needed to implement a tree structure (or really any data-oriented system). In earlier chapters of the book, I mostly talked about techniques to load data en masse. Those techniques will still work to load a tree, but in this chapter, I want to build a slightly more realistic example that simulates users creating data. (If your users are creating 20,000 nodes an hour in your objects, you are going to need a lot bigger server than I am working with very quickly!)

In a tree, since the typical requirement is that every tree have only one root node, the insert procedure will include the method to link the new node to another node in the tree.

Doing this process one row at a time is more like you will see in the real world because data changes over time. Seeing how long it takes to generate thousands of rows may be an important part of determining which algorithm to use when building a tree structure. It really depends on your individual needs. Graph nodes, particularly those in a tree structure in a natural, one-at-a-time manner, are not necessarily as rapidly added to a data structure as normal rows that are independent from other rows.

```
CREATE OR ALTER PROCEDURE SqlGraph.Company$Insert
(
    @Name VARCHAR(20),
         --using natural key values to be a bit more natural
    @ParentCompanyName VARCHAR(20)
         --and to make sure surrogate values needn't always
         --be the same in demo code
)
AS
BEGIN
    SET NOCOUNT ON;
     BEGIN TRY
        BEGIN TRANSACTION
           --fetch the parent of the node
           DECLARE @ParentNode NVARCHAR(1000) =
                     (SELECT $node_id
                      FROM SqlGraph.Company
                      WHERE name = @ParentCompanyName);
```

```
    IF @ParentCompanyName IS NOT NULL
                    AND @ParentNode IS NULL
      THROW 50000, 'Invalid ParentCompanyName', 1;
    ELSE
      BEGIN
            --insert done by simply using the Name of the
            --parent to get the key of
            --the parent...

            IF @ParentNode IS NULL
              BEGIN
                --there are places where it is
                --advantageous to know what node is the
                --root node especially since we will
                --generally, just want one.
                INSERT INTO SqlGraph.Company
                                (Name, RootNodeFlag)
              SELECT @Name,1;
                END
              ELSE
              BEGIN
                INSERT INTO SqlGraph.Company(Name)
                SELECT @Name;
                DECLARE @ChildNode nvarchar(1000) =
                                (SELECT $node_id
                                 FROM SqlGraph.Company
                                 WHERE name = @Name);

                INSERT INTO SqlGraph.ReportsTo
                                ($from_id, $to_id)
                VALUES (@ParentNode, @ChildNode);
            END;
        END
        COMMIT TRANSACTION
END TRY
BEGIN CATCH
```

```
                IF XACT_STATE() <> 0
                    ROLLBACK TRANSACTION;
                THROW; --just rethrow the error
        END CATCH;

END;
GO
```

In the following script, you will insert the first set of nodes to implement the subgraph shown in Figure 5-2.

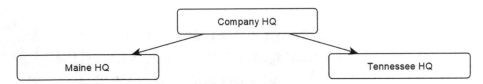

Figure 5-2. *Structure you will have after the first inserts*

```
EXEC SqlGraph.Company$Insert @Name = 'Company HQ',
                             @ParentCompanyName = NULL;

EXEC SqlGraph.Company$Insert @Name = 'Maine HQ',
                             @ParentCompanyName = 'Company HQ';

EXEC SqlGraph.Company$Insert @Name = 'Tennessee HQ',
                             @ParentCompanyName = 'Company HQ';
```

Looking at the data that was just inserted:

```
SELECT CAST($node_id AS VARCHAR(64)) AS [$node_id],
       CompanyId,
       Name
FROM SqlGraph.Company;

SELECT CAST($edge_id as varchar(64)) as [$edge_id],
       CAST($from_id as varchar(64)) as [$from_id],
       CAST($to_id as varchar(64)) as [$to_id]
FROM   SqlGraph.ReportsTo;
```

What you will see is that the data is hard to display in a book (it really isn't that easy to look at when you are working with it either! I just let it wrap for this example).

$node_id	CompanyId	Name
{"type":"node","schema":"SqlGraph","table":"Company","id":0}	1	Company HQ
{"type":"node","schema":"SqlGraph","table":"Company","id":1}	2	Maine HQ
{"type":"node","schema":"SqlGraph","table":"Company","id":2}	3	Tennessee HQ

And the edges:

```
$edge_id                                                         $from_id
                                                                 $to_id
--------------------------------------------------------------------------------
{"type":"edge","schema":"SqlGraph","table":"ReportsTo","id":0}
{"type":"node","schema":"SqlGraph","table":"Company","id":0}
{"type":"node","schema":"SqlGraph","table":"Company","id":1}

{"type":"edge","schema":"SqlGraph","table":"ReportsTo","id":1}
{"type":"node","schema":"SqlGraph","table":"Company","id":0}
{"type":"node","schema":"SqlGraph","table":"Company","id":2}
```

Rather than even try to output data and try to format it in its natural style, for most of the book, when I need to show the internals, I will use the following functions that are available in a tools file in the downloads for this chapter:

```
SELECT Tools.Graph$NodeIdFormat($node_id,0) AS [$node_id],
       CompanyId,
       Name
FROM SqlGraph.Company;

SELECT Tools.Graph$EdgeIdFormat($edge_id,0) AS [$edge_id],
       Tools.Graph$NodeIdFormat($from_id,0) AS [$from_id],
       Tools.Graph$NodeIdFormat($to_id,0) AS [$to_id]
FROM SqlGraph.ReportsTo;
```

This returns the same details in a more compact manner, due to the limited real estate on the page. I set the second parameter in the function call to 0 to not include schemas in this example to save space since all tables involved will be in the same schema.

```
$node_id         CompanyId    Name
---------------  -----------  --------------------
Company id:0     1           Company HQ
Company id:1     2           Maine HQ
Company id:2     3           Tennessee HQ

$edge_id          $from_id         $to_id
----------------  ---------------  --------------
ReportsTo id:0    Company id:0     Company id:1
ReportsTo id:1    Company id:0     Company id:2
```

You will see that you have three nodes and two edges. CompanyHQ's internal id value is 0 assuming you don't have any error/retries along the way (I did many times and started over so I could get the ideal output). The internal values are not that important even to my examples, so it is not imperative that these are the internal values you see when you execute this code.

Next, you are going to add your first leaf node. To make the whole example simpler, I only put sale data on root nodes. This is also a very reasonable expectation to have in the real world for many situations. It does not really affect the outcome if sale data was appended to the non-root nodes either, but it would be very typical for the stores or salespersons to have sales, but the region to only have sales based on the stores or salespersons.

```
EXEC SqlGraph.Company$Insert @Name = 'Nashville Branch',
                    @ParentCompanyName = 'Tennessee HQ';
EXEC SqlGraph.Sale$InsertTestData @Name = 'Nashville Branch';
```

After executing that code, you can see the sale data inserted here:

```
SELECT *
FROM   SqlGraph.Sale;
```

This returns

```
SalesId  TransactionNumber Amount    CompanyId
-------- ----------------- --------- -----------
1        1                 0.25      4
2        2                 0.50      4
3        3                 0.75      4
4        4                 1.00      4
5        5                 1.25      4
```

The goal is that every time you generate this set (and later when you build other versions of this test database), Nashville Branch will always have the same $3.75 worth of sales. Obviously, this is not a very real amount of money (and every new node will have five new sales that are always increasing), but keeping values and row counts the same is helpful for a performance and correctness test.

The fact that values match in examples has saved me many times when testing the tree algorithms (which, as you will see in the next chapter, can occasionally be kind of hairy). I use this set of data as my unit test for all these algorithms. Using this query, you can see the values in the table:

```
SELECT Name, SUM(amount)
FROM   SqlGraph.Sale
          JOIN SqlGraph.Company
             ON Company.CompanyId = Sale.CompanyId
GROUP BY Name;
```

This shows you just the one row:

```
Name
-------------------- ---------------------------------------
Nashville Branch     3.75
```

Now insert the rest of the data for the graph, adding sales for all of the leaf nodes:

```
EXEC SqlGraph.Company$Insert @Name = 'Knoxville Branch',
     @ParentCompanyName = 'Tennessee HQ';

EXEC SqlGraph.Sale$InsertTestData @Name = 'Knoxville Branch';
```

```
EXEC SqlGraph.Company$Insert @Name = 'Memphis Branch',
     @ParentCompanyName = 'Tennessee HQ';

EXEC SqlGraph.Sale$InsertTestData @Name = 'Memphis Branch';

EXEC SqlGraph.Company$Insert @Name = 'Portland Branch',
     @ParentCompanyName = 'Maine HQ';

EXEC SqlGraph.Sale$InsertTestData @Name = 'Portland Branch';

EXEC SqlGraph.Company$Insert @Name = 'Camden Branch',
     @ParentCompanyName = 'Maine HQ';

EXEC SqlGraph.Sale$InsertTestData @Name = 'Camden Branch';
GO
```

Now let's look at the data in a very human-readable form. One of the interesting things about SQL graph queries is that there is no easy way to do an OUTER style join/connection with the syntax. So, if you want to list all the data in the tree, you need to do a little bit more than just the MATCH query to get the root node in the output. The root node(s) in the table turn out to be the ones where the $node_id doesn't appear as a $to_id in an edge.

It is something you will also need to do in any graph, but it is very much a part of the process when building a tree. Avoiding that query is why I added the RootNodeFlag column to my objects.

The following query will give you the nodes in the tree including the root:

```
--get the root
SELECT Company.CompanyId, Company.Name, NULL AS ParentCompanyId
FROM   SqlGraph.Company
WHERE  RootNodeFlag = 1
UNION ALL
--get all the children of the root. Our tree can only have the one root
since we have a UNIQUE constraint on the $to_id column
SELECT Company.CompanyId, Company.Name, ParentCompany.CompanyId AS
ParentCompanyId
```

```
FROM    SqlGraph.Company,
        SqlGraph.ReportsTo,
        SqlGraph.Company AS ParentCompany
WHERE MATCH(Company<-(ReportsTo)-ParentCompany);
```

This returns

CompanyId	Name	ParentCompanyId
1	Company HQ	NULL
2	Maine HQ	1
3	Tennessee HQ	1
4	Nashville Branch	3
5	Knoxville Branch	3
6	Memphis Branch	3
7	Portland Branch	2
8	Camden Branch	2

In the downloads, I compiled this to a view named SqlGraph.CompanyClean to make continuing queries to these structures easier to work with.

Next up are few operations for how to look at the data in a semi-graphical manner. In the following query, you output the data as a hierarchy, showing the path through the tree (I commented out the Name column, as it is also represented at the last value in the hierarchy):

```
--the first node in a query will typically not show up in
--the output, so we have to include it seperately
SELECT 0 AS Level, Company.Name AS Hierarchy --,Company.Name
FROM   SqlGraph.Company
WHERE  RootNodeFlag = 1

UNION ALL

SELECT    COUNT(ReportsToCompany.CompanyId)
                    WITHIN GROUP (GRAPH PATH) ,
          Company.NAME + '->' +
          STRING_AGG(ReportsToCompany.name, '->')
                    WITHIN GROUP (GRAPH PATH) AS Friends
```

```
          --,LAST_VALUE(ReportsToCompany.name)
          --          WITHIN GROUP (GRAPH PATH) AS LastNode
FROM    SqlGraph.Company AS Company,
        SqlGraph.ReportsTo FOR PATH AS ReportsTo,
        SqlGraph.Company FOR PATH AS ReportsToCompany
WHERE MATCH(SHORTEST_PATH(Company(-(ReportsTo)
                                        ->ReportsToCompany)+))
 AND  Company.RootNodeFlag = 1
```

The output of this query gives the following:

```
Level        Hierarchy
-----------  -------------------------------------------------
0            Company HQ
1            Company HQ->Maine HQ
1            Company HQ->Tennessee HQ
2            Company HQ->Tennessee HQ->Nashville Branch
2            Company HQ->Tennessee HQ->Knoxville Branch
2            Company HQ->Tennessee HQ->Memphis Branch
2            Company HQ->Maine HQ->Portland Branch
2            Company HQ->Maine HQ->Camden Branch;
```

Using this output (plus including the Name column), you make that a CTE and then use the level column to indent each item, and the Hierarchy column to sort by:

```
WITH BaseRows AS
(
SELECT 0 AS Level, Company.Name AS Hierarchy ,Company.Name
FROM  SqlGraph.Company
WHERE RootNodeFlag = 1

UNION ALL

SELECT  COUNT(ReportsToCompany.CompanyId)
                      WITHIN GROUP (GRAPH PATH) ,
     Company.NAME + '->' +
     STRING_AGG(ReportsToCompany.name, '->')
                      WITHIN GROUP (GRAPH PATH) AS Friends
```

```
          ,LAST_VALUE(ReportsToCompany.name)
                        WITHIN GROUP (GRAPH PATH) AS LastNode
FROM   SqlGraph.Company AS Company,
       SqlGraph.ReportsTo FOR PATH AS ReportsTo,
       SqlGraph.Company FOR PATH AS ReportsToCompany
WHERE MATCH(SHORTEST_PATH(Company(-(ReportsTo)
                               ->ReportsToCompany)+))
   AND Company.RootNodeFlag = 1
)
SELECT REPLICATE('--> ',Level) + Name AS HierarchyDisplay
FROM   BaseRows
ORDER BY Hierarchy;
```

This returns the following output:

```
HierarchyDisplay
-----------------------------------------
Company HQ
--> Maine HQ
--> --> Camden Branch
--> --> Portland Branch
--> Tennessee HQ
--> --> Knoxville Branch
--> --> Memphis Branch
--> --> Nashville Branch
```

Finding ways to output the hierarchy in a readable format is a large part of the battle of working with graph functionality, since there are really no easy ways to output the data graphically. SHORTEST_PATH works perfectly for tree structures because every node can appear exactly once in the output. In the last two chapters of the book, I cover the limitations of SHORTEST_PATH that we have to deal with in cyclic graphs, but for trees it is perfect because the shortest path from one node to another is, by definition, always one path.

In the downloads, I made this into a view named SqlGraph.CompanyHierarchyDisp lay, which I will use to output the examples in the rest of the chapter. In it I include the Hierarchy, Level and Name columns just to give a bit more information in places where it turns out to be useful (also the Hierarchy column is used to sort the output).

Reparenting Nodes

Once you have your data into the tree structure, a common operation you might need to do a tree is to move one node to be a child of a different node. This is a very typical thing to do in something like a managerial relationship object.

Reparenting a node in a tree using an adjacency list type of structure (storing the edges in a simple from-to object like SQL Graph does) is generally simple. Just modify the $from_id value from one parent to another.

This is how it will be accomplished with SQL Graph edges, except you cannot modify the edge object's $from_id or $to_id values, so you need to delete the original edge and create a new one. If you have data stored in the edge object, you need to handle that in your code as well (if the data makes sense where you reparent the row to, obviously).

For multi-step processes in T-SQL code, it is always good to use a stored procedure, which makes it a lot easier to use a transaction in a safe manner where you know it will be committed or rolled back. Doing this in your ad-hoc style code multiple times is a lot more cumbersome than a stored procedure and more prone to errors like forgetting to commit the transaction and losing work.

In the next bit of code, you implement the reparent code for the Company object. Reparenting with an adjacency list type structure can be thought of as an edge update operation, but I generally implement it separately from a general update procedure because I typically want to update something like the notes about the connection of two nodes independently from moving them to a different location in the tree. Hence the security on the reparent operation is likely to be different than the normal update.

The following code implements the reparent operation. (If you have any columns on your edge object, you need to make sure and copy those attributes in the code as well, since a reparent requires you to delete the existing edge and reinsert the row.)

```
CREATE OR ALTER PROCEDURE SqlGraph.Company$Reparent
(
    @Name varchar(20), --again using natural key values
    @NewParentCompanyName varchar(20)
)
AS
BEGIN
    SET NOCOUNT ON;
    BEGIN TRY;
    BEGIN TRANSACTION;
```

```
          --get the new location you wish to change to
                    --the from is what is changing
          DECLARE @FromId nvarchar(1000),
                  @ToId nvarchar(1000) --to id will not change

          --use the natural key values to fetch the $from_id/$to_id
          SELECT @FromId = $node_id
          FROM   SqlGraph.Company
          WHERE  name = @NewParentCompanyName;

          SELECT @ToId = $node_id
          FROM   SqlGraph.Company
          WHERE  name = @Name;

          --Delete the old edge, and since this isn't changing
          --it will remain the same (note, $to_id is unique, so
          --no need to worry with the old $from_id value
          DELETE SqlGraph.ReportsTo
          WHERE  $to_id = @ToId;

          --create a new edge
          INSERT INTO SqlGraph.ReportsTo($From_id, $to_id)
          VALUES (@FromId, @ToId);

          --finish up
          COMMIT TRANSACTION;
          END TRY
          BEGIN CATCH
                    IF XACT_STATE() <> 0
                            ROLLBACK TRANSACTION;
                    THROW; --just rethrow the error
          END CATCH;
END;
```

Now, let's look at the tree structure as it is currently:

```
SELECT HierarchyDisplay
FROM SqlGraph.CompanyHierarchyDisplay
ORDER BY Hierarchy;
```

This returns

```
HierarchyDisplay
--------------------------------
Company HQ
--> Maine HQ
--> --> Camden Branch
--> --> Portland Branch
--> Tennessee HQ
--> --> Knoxville Branch
--> --> Memphis Branch
--> --> Nashville Branch
```

Now let's reparent Maine HQ to be under Tennessee HQ:

```
EXEC SqlGraph.Company$Reparent @Name = 'Maine HQ',
                    @NewParentCompanyName = 'Tennessee HQ';
```

After execution, looking at the code, you can now see that Maine HQ is a child of Tennessee HQ. This query of the view now returns

```
HierarchyDisplay
-----------------------------------------
Company HQ
--> Tennessee HQ
--> --> Knoxville Branch
--> --> Maine HQ
--> --> --> Camden Branch
--> --> --> Portland Branch
--> --> Memphis Branch
--> --> Nashville Branch
```

Note also that all the child rows of Maine HQ come along for the ride. I won't implement it here, but you could "somewhat less easily" just remove the node from the tree and insert it into the structure. This would require shuffling all the child nodes to the parent of the item you are removing. This is a less-likely use case and could be done using multiple reparents when desired. (The delete code will implement something similar, since it is typical in that scenario, so you could adapt that code if needed).

Now put `Maine HQ` back where it belongs using the following code:

```
EXEC SQLGraph.Company$Reparent @Name = 'Maine HQ',
                @NewParentCompanyName = 'Company HQ';
```

Then check for yourself that it is back into the right location.

Deleting a Node

Next up, you will implement the ability to delete a node. Deletes are somewhat more interesting than reparenting because if you delete a node that has child nodes in the structure, what do you do? Do you just try to delete that node? Or delete the child rows? In this section, you will implement a procedure that handles three possibilities:

1. Delete if the node is a leaf node, with no issues.

2. If the node is a parent to other nodes, do one of the following:

   a. Delete all of the child nodes.

   b. Move child nodes to the parent of the node being deleted. Unlike reparenting a node, deleting a node **does** feel like it is necessary to handle the one item delete (for example, if Manager X is removed, their employees are moved to Manager X's manager until a new one is found).

Note   You could set up other possibilities pretty easily, like replacing the node or moving the child rows to another node represented by another variable in the parameter. This could be added to the stored procedures provided, but I will not add that for brevity's sake.

These possibilities are implemented with three parameters: the name of the node to delete, one to say if you should attempt to delete the child nodes, and one to reparent any child nodes that exist. This code is very long, but it is commented to explain how the delete operations are being done.

```
CREATE OR ALTER PROCEDURE SqlGraph.Company$Delete
    @Name       varchar(20),
    @DeleteChildNodesFlag bit = 0,
    @ReparentChildNodesToParentFlag BIT = 0
```

```
AS

BEGIN
    SET NOCOUNT ON;
    BEGIN TRY;

    IF @DeleteChildNodesFlag = 1 AND
                    @ReparentChildNodesToParentFlag = 1
        THROW 50000,'Both @DeleteChildNodesFlag and (wrap)
         @ReparentChildNodesToParentFlag cannot be set to 1', 1;

    IF @DeleteChildNodesFlag = 1
    BEGIN

            --use this to get all the children of
            --node to be deleted
            --we need not only the direct descendants (which we
            --will use for reparenting the
            --child rows), but their descendants too so we can
            --delete everything.
            SELECT  LAST_VALUE(ReportsTo.$to_id)
                 WITHIN GROUP (GRAPH PATH) AS  CompanyNodeId
            INTO    #deleteThese
            FROM    SqlGraph.Company AS Company,
                        SqlGraph.ReportsTo FOR PATH AS ReportsTo,
                        SqlGraph.Company FOR PATH
                                            AS ReportsToCompany
            WHERE MATCH(SHORTEST_PATH(Company(-(ReportsTo)
                                        ->ReportsToCompany)+))
              AND Company.Name = @name

            --this is the node that was originally requested to
            --be deleted
            INSERT INTO #deleteThese
            SELECT $node_id
            FROM SqlGraph.Company
            WHERE name = @Name;
```

```
    --Now remove all traces of the parent and children
    --as a from or a to in a relationship, then remove the
    --company rows.
  BEGIN TRANSACTION;

  DELETE SqlGraph.ReportsTo
  WHERE  $from_id IN (SELECT CompanyNodeId
                      FROM #deleteThese);

  DELETE SqlGraph.ReportsTo
  WHERE  $to_id IN (SELECT CompanyNodeId
                    FROM #deleteThese);

  DELETE SqlGraph.Company
  WHERE  $Node_id IN (SELECT CompanyNodeId
                      FROM  #deleteThese);

  COMMIT TRANSACTION;

END;
ELSE IF @ReparentChildNodesToParentFlag = 1
BEGIN

  --fetch the direct decendents of the row to reparent
  SELECT $to_id AS ToId
  INTO   #reparentThese
  FROM   SqlGraph.ReportsTo

WHERE  $from_id = (SELECT $node_Id
                   FROM  SqlGraph.Company
                   WHERE  Name = @Name)

--this gets the parent row where you will move the child rows
 --to. Would not work to remove the root
  DECLARE @NewFromId NVARCHAR(1000) = (
                   SELECT $from_id
                   FROM   SqlGraph.ReportsTo
                   WHERE  $to_id= (SELECT $node_Id
                                   FROM  SqlGraph.Company
                                   WHERE   Name = @Name));
```

```
    --delete the reporting rows for the rows to be
        -- reparented
    DELETE FROM SqlGraph.ReportsTo
    WHERE  $to_id IN (SELECT ToId FROM #reparentThese)

    --delete reporting rows for the row to be deleted
    DELETE FROM SqlGraph.ReportsTo
    WHERE  $to_id IN (SELECT $node_Id
                            FROM   SqlGraph.Company
                            WHERE  Name = @Name)

    --if the parent is not null, create new rows
     IF @NewFromId IS NOT NULL
            INSERT INTO SqlGraph.ReportsTo
            (
              $from_id, $to_id
            )
            SELECT @NewFromId, ToId
            FROM    #reparentThese
      ELSE
         THROW 50000,
              'The parent row did not exist, operation fails'
                    ,1;

    --delete the company
    DELETE FROM SqlGraph.Company
    WHERE  $node_id = (SELECT $node_Id
                            FROM   SqlGraph.Company
                            WHERE  Name = @Name)

    END
  ELSE
    BEGIN
    --we are trusting the edge and foreign key constraint
    --to make sure that there are no orphaned rows
    DECLARE @CompanyNodeId nvarchar(1000)
```

```
    --fetch the node id of the company
    SELECT @CompanyNodeId = $node_id
    FROM    SqlGraph.Company
    WHERE   name = @Name

    --try to delete it
    BEGIN TRANSACTION

    DELETE SqlGraph.ReportsTo
    WHERE   $to_id = @CompanyNodeId;

    DELETE SqlGraph.Company
    WHERE $node_id = @CompanyNodeId;

    COMMIT TRANSACTION


  END;

 END TRY
 BEGIN CATCH
   IF XACT_STATE() <> 0
       ROLLBACK TRANSACTION;
   THROW; --just rethrow the error
 END CATCH;
END;
```

To test this code, add new nodes in the graph structures, as seen in Figure 5-3.

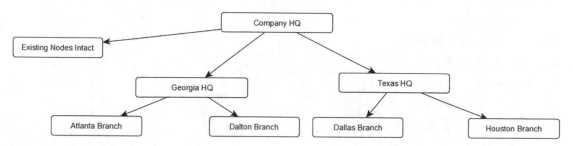

Figure 5-3. *New nodes that will be added to the data structures*

```
--add a few rows to test the delete. No activity rows
--because that would limit deletes in a way that is
--immaterial to the example
EXEC SqlGraph.Company$Insert @Name = 'Georgia HQ',
                    @ParentCompanyName = 'Company HQ';
EXEC SqlGraph.Company$Insert @Name = 'Atlanta Branch',
                    @ParentCompanyName = 'Georgia HQ';
EXEC SqlGraph.Company$Insert @Name = 'Dalton Branch',
                    @ParentCompanyName = 'Georgia HQ';
EXEC SqlGraph.Company$Insert @Name = 'Texas HQ',
                    @ParentCompanyName = 'Company HQ';
EXEC SqlGraph.Company$Insert @Name = 'Dallas Branch',
                    @ParentCompanyName = 'Texas HQ';
EXEC SqlGraph.Company$Insert @Name = 'Houston Branch',
                    @ParentCompanyName = 'Texas HQ';
```

Now, look at the nodes in the tree:

```
SELECT HierarchyDisplay
FROM SqlGraph.CompanyHierarchyDisplay
ORDER BY Hierarchy;
```

The hierarchy now looks like this:

```
HierarchyDisplay
-----------------------------------------
Company HQ
--> Georgia HQ
--> --> Atlanta Branch
--> --> Dalton Branch
--> Maine HQ
--> --> Camden Branch
--> --> Portland Branch
--> Tennessee HQ
--> --> Knoxville Branch
--> --> Memphis Branch
--> --> Nashville Branch
```

```
--> Texas HQ
--> --> Dallas Branch
--> --> Houston Branch
```

Try to delete Georgia HQ using only the default parameters (leaving children rows alone) using the following call:

```
EXEC SqlGraph.Company$Delete @Name = 'Georgia HQ';
```

Because you created the edge constraint as NO ACTION, when you try to delete the parent node, this operation fails with the following error message:

```
Msg 547, Level 16, State 0, Procedure SqlGraph.Company$Delete, Line 60
The DELETE statement conflicted with the EDGE REFERENCE constraint
"EC_ReportsTo$DefinesParentOf". The conflict occurred in database
"GraphDBTests", table "SqlGraph.ReportsTo".
```

If you try to delete a leaf node, it works because it has no dependencies in the graph.

```
--Delete Atlanta
EXEC SqlGraph.Company$Delete @Name = 'Atlanta Branch';
```

Check the structure and you will see the Atlanta Branch row is gone. Next, try the deleting child rows along with the node you specifically name:

```
EXEC SqlGraph.Company$Delete @Name = 'Georgia HQ',
                             @DeleteChildNodesFlag = 1;
```

Now you will see that the Georgia HQ and Dalton Branch rows are both gone.

```
HierarchyDisplay
----------------------------------------
Company HQ
--> Maine HQ
--> --> Camden Branch
--> --> Portland Branch
--> Tennessee HQ
--> --> Knoxville Branch
--> --> Memphis Branch
--> --> Nashville Branch
```

```
--> Texas HQ
--> --> Dallas Branch
--> --> Houston Branch
```

Next, let's see what the @ReparentChildNodesToParentFlag does. Executing the following code removes the Texas HQ row, but now the Dallas Branch and Houston Branch nodes will be moved up as child nodes of the Company HQ node.

```
EXEC SqlGraph.Company$Delete @Name = 'Texas HQ',
                @ReparentChildNodesToParentFlag = 1;
```

Viewing the data, you can see that Dallas Branch and Houston Branch nodes are now child nodes of Company HQ:

```
HierarchyDisplay
-----------------------------------------------
Company HQ
--> Dallas Branch
--> Houston Branch
--> Maine HQ
--> --> Camden Branch
--> --> Portland Branch
--> Tennessee HQ
--> --> Knoxville Branch
--> --> Memphis Branch
--> --> Nashville Branch
```

Finally, clean up the nodes that are left over from this example:

```
EXEC SqlGraph.Company$Delete @Name = 'Dallas Branch';
EXEC SqlGraph.Company$Delete @Name = 'Houston Branch';
```

Tree Output Code

In this section, you will learn additional techniques that are handy when working with a tree structure. Each will be coded into an object and will (not coincidentally) be the basis of the performance testing code that you will use in the next chapter with far larger data sets than you have worked with in here.

The procedures will do the following actions:

- **Return part of the tree**: This will extend the functionality of the CompanyHierarchyDisplay view that was created in the chapter to let you pick the starting node and then return the nodes that are below it.

- **Determine if a child node exists**: This is a very typical piece of code that you will need when building security applications. You want to know if a node exists in the tree at any level.

- **Aggregate child activity at every level**: Summing up sales activity of all the child nodes of every node in the tree, from root to leaf.

Returning Part of the Tree

This table-valued user defined function is an extension of the view created earlier in the chapter. The difference is that it lets you start at a specific node rather than always returning the entire tree.

```
CREATE OR ALTER FUNCTION SqlGraph.Company$ReturnHierarchy
(
    @CompanyName varchar(20)
)
RETURNS @Output TABLE (CompanyId INT, Name VARCHAR(20),
                    Level INT, Hierarchy NVARCHAR(4000),
                    IdHierarchy NVARCHAR(4000),
                    HierarchyDisplay NVARCHAR(4000))
AS
BEGIN
    --get the identifier for the node you want to start with
    DECLARE @CompanyId int, @NodeName nvarchar(max)
    SELECT  @CompanyId = CompanyId,
            @Nodename = Name
    FROM    SqlGraph.Company
    WHERE   Name = @CompanyName;
```

```
;WITH baseRows as
 (
--include node that you are looking for
SELECT @companyId as CompanyId, @NodeName as Name,
        1 as Level,
        '\' + Cast(@companyId as nvarchar(10)) + '\' as
                IdHierarchy, --\ delimited but with id num
          '\' + @NodeName AS Hieararchy
UNION ALL
SELECT
        LAST_VALUE(ToCompany.CompanyId)
                WITHIN GROUP (GRAPH PATH) AS CompanyId,
        LAST_VALUE(ToCompany.Name)
                WITHIN GROUP (GRAPH PATH) AS NodeName,
        1+COUNT(ToCompany.Name)
                WITHIN GROUP (GRAPH PATH) AS levels,
        '\' + CAST(FromCompany.CompanyId as NVARCHAR(10))+
        '\' + STRING_AGG(cast(ToCompany.CompanyId as
                                        nvarchar(10)), '\')
          WITHIN GROUP (GRAPH PATH) + '\' AS Idhierarchy,

        '\' +  FromCompany.NAME + '\' +
        STRING_AGG(ToCompany.Name, '\')
            WITHIN GROUP (GRAPH PATH) + '\' AS hierarchy

FROM
        SqlGraph.Company AS FromCompany,
        SqlGraph.ReportsTo FOR PATH AS ReportsTo,
        SqlGraph.Company FOR PATH AS ToCompany
WHERE
      MATCH(SHORTEST_PATH(FromCompany(-(ReportsTo)
                                        ->ToCompany)+))
    --start the processing from the parameter's companyId
        AND FromCompany.CompanyId = @companyId
 )
```

```
        INSERT INTO @Output
        SELECT *, REPLICATE('--> ',LEVEL - 1) + Name
                                        AS HierarchyDisplay
        FROM  BaseRows
RETURN;

END;
```

If you want to see just the Tennessee HQ tree of data, you can use

```
SELECT *
FROM    SqlGraph.Company$ReturnHierarchy('Tennessee HQ');
```

This returns three rows with the same output as the view did just showing the subtree.

Determining If a Child Node Exists

The following procedure will let you ask, for one company, if this is a child of another company row. This is useful in many cases, for example in security when you start to have inherited group rights. Then you can see if a user is a member of a group at any level of inheritance.

```
CREATE OR ALTER FUNCTION SqlGraph.Company$CheckForChild
(
        @CompanyName varchar(20),
        @CheckForChildOfCompanyName varchar(20)
)
RETURNS bit
AS
BEGIN
        --get the id value of the company to check for
        DECLARE @CompanyId INT, @ChildFlag BIT = 0;
        SELECT @CompanyId = CompanyId
        FROM    SqlGraph.Company
        WHERE   Name = @CompanyName;
```

```
    --get the id of the company to see if it is a child of
    DECLARE @CheckForChildOfCompanyId int;
    SELECT  @CheckForChildOfCompanyId = CompanyId
    FROM    SqlGraph.Company
    WHERE   Name = @CheckForChildOfCompanyName;

    --query the structure
    ;WITH baseRows AS
     (
    --gets the relations to @checkForChildOfCompanyId
    SELECT LAST_VALUE(ToCompany.CompanyId) WITHIN GROUP
                                (GRAPH PATH) AS ChildCompanyId
    FROM
            SqlGraph.Company AS FromCompany,
            SqlGraph.ReportsTo FOR PATH AS ReportsTo,
            SqlGraph.Company FOR PATH AS ToCompany
    WHERE  MATCH(SHORTEST_PATH(FromCompany(-(ReportsTo)
                                        ->ToCompany)+))
      AND FromCompany.CompanyId = @CheckForChildOfCompanyId
     )
    --then filter to see if the passed in row matches
    SELECT @ChildFlag = 1
    FROM  BaseRows
    WHERE childCompanyId = @CompanyId;
RETURN @ChildFlag;

END;
```

Knowing the data, you now have (using the new function from the last section)

```
SELECT HierarchyDisplay
FROM    SqlGraph.Company$ReturnHierarchy('Company HQ' )
ORDER BY Hierarchy;
```

that returns

```
HierarchyDisplay
-------------------------------
Company HQ
--> Maine HQ
--> --> Portland Branch
--> --> Camden Branch
--> Tennessee HQ
--> --> Nashville Branch
--> --> Knoxville Branch
--> --> Memphis Branch
```

You can test the function this way. Check several scenarios with Camden Branch as the basis:

```
SELECT (CASE SqlGraph.Company$CheckForChild
                    ('Camden Branch','Company HQ')
        WHEN 1 THEN 'Yes' ELSE 'No' END)
                                    AS Camden_to_Company,
       (CASE SqlGraph.Company$CheckForChild
                    ('Camden Branch','Maine HQ')
        WHEN 1 THEN 'Yes' ELSE 'No' END) AS Camden_to_Maine,
       (CASE SqlGraph.Company$CheckForChild
                    ('Camden Branch','Tennessee HQ')
        WHEN 1 THEN 'Yes' ELSE 'No' END)
                                    AS Camden_to_Tennessee;
```

This returns

```
Camden_to_Company Camden_to_Maine Camden_to_Tennessee
----------------- --------------- -------------------
Yes               Yes             No
```

As you can see, Camden Branch is a child to Company HQ and Maine HQ, but not Tennessee Branch. In the next chapter, you will use this function on a few different implementations of trees to compare how much time each takes in much larger trees.

Aggregating Child Activity at Every Level

The next code to be implement is the ability to aggregate over the tree. For example, say you have the following sales figures:

```
Company HQ
--> Maine HQ
--> --> Portland Branch   $1
--> --> Camden Branch     $1
--> Tennessee HQ
--> --> Nashville Branch $1
--> --> Knoxville Branch $1
--> --> Memphis Branch    $1
```

You need to be able to not only say that the leaf nodes had $1 each sales; you also need to say that Tennessee HQ had $3 in sales, Maine $2, and the overall organization had $5 in sales. Looking at the hierarchy in the text above, you might think this is a pretty simple operation (and it is, relatively, but it is a decent bit of code that needs explanation).

Just fetch the hierarchy's lower level, then get the parents and sum up, and then the next parents and sum up. The problem is, hierarchies are rarely so balanced in the real world and probably not that shallow (most likely, your real scenario is going to add in sales staff and their sales, too, which will make for a bit more challenging implementation).

The way to process this is to take a recursive operation and then flip it into a relational process.

The basis of this operation is what I have coined an *expanded hierarchy* (I learned the foundational technique in Ralph Kimball's Data Warehousing course. More about the Kimball helper table method in the next chapter.) This is basically taking every node that is a parent in the hierarchy and fetching their entire hierarchy. It uses code you used before to get all of the children of a row, but instead of filtering to one node, you return the hierarchy for *every* node. Then every node will have all of their child rows added to the output/table.

For example, take the following subgraph of the tree:

```
--> Tennessee HQ
--> --> Nashville Branch $1
--> --> Knoxville Branch $1
--> --> Memphis Branch    $1
```

The code is going to output this expanded hierarchy that looks like this:

```
CompanyName            IncludesCompanyName
--------------------   --------------------
Tennessee HQ           Tennessee HQ
Tennessee HQ           Nashville Branch
Tennessee HQ           Knoxville Branch
Tennessee HQ           Memphis Branch
Nashville Branch       Nashville Branch
Knoxville Branch       Knoxville Branch
Memphis Branch         Memphis Branch
```

With this set of data, you can join to the activity using the IncludesCompanyName to get the activity sum, and then you can group by the CompanyName column to get the sales of the different nodes. The number of rows output by this can be considerable, but as you will see in the next chapter, even with 200,000+ nodes, it is not too much for even my desktop computer to handle.

```
CREATE OR ALTER PROCEDURE SqlGraph.Company$ReportSales
    @DisplayFromNodeName VARCHAR(20)
AS
BEGIN

--output the Expanded Hierarchy...
WITH ExpandedHierarchy (ParentCompanyId, ChildCompanyId)
AS (
    --gets all of the nodes of the hierarchy
    SELECT Company.CompanyId AS ParentCompanyId,
           Company.CompanyId AS ChildCompanyId
    FROM SqlGraph.Company

UNION ALL
```

```
    --joins back to the CTE to recursively retrieve the rows
    --note that TreeLevel is incremented on each iteration
    SELECT ExpandedHierarchy.ParentCompanyId,
           ToCompany.CompanyId
    FROM ExpandedHierarchy,
         SqlGraph.Company AS FromCompany,
         SqlGraph.ReportsTo,
         SqlGraph.Company AS ToCompany
    WHERE ExpandedHierarchy.ChildCompanyId = FromCompany.CompanyId
          AND MATCH(FromCompany-(ReportsTo)->ToCompany)
),
--using the hierarchy returning function, get only the nodes
--that you desire
FilterAndSweeten AS
(
      SELECT ExpandedHierarchy.*,
             CompanyHierarchyDisplay.Hierarchy,
             CompanyHierarchyDisplay.HierarchyDisplay,
             CompanyHierarchyDisplay.Name

      FROM   ExpandedHierarchy
           JOIN [SqlGraph].[Company$ReturnHierarchy]
               (@DisplayFromNodeName) AS CompanyHierarchyDisplay
             ON CompanyHierarchyDisplay.CompanyId =
                          ExpandedHierarchy.ParentCompanyId
)
,--get totals for each Company for the aggregate
    CompanyTotals
AS (SELECT CompanyId,
           SUM(cast(Amount as decimal(20,2))) AS TotalAmount
    FROM SqlGraph.Sale
    GROUP BY CompanyId),
--aggregate each Company for the Company
```

```
    Aggregations AS
    --perform the math that gives every node their sums
    (SELECT FilterAndSweeten.ParentCompanyId,
            SUM(CompanyTotals.TotalAmount) AS TotalSalesAmount,
            --these are unique and could be in the GROUP BY,
            --but this works great and makes it clear we are
            --grouping on the ParentCompanyId only
            MAX(hierarchy) AS Hierarchy,
            MAX(hierarchyDisplay) AS HierarchyDisplay,
            MAX(Name) as Name
     FROM FilterAndSweeten
         JOIN CompanyTotals
            ON CompanyTotals.CompanyId =
                        FilterAndSweeten.ChildCompanyId
     GROUP BY FilterAndSweeten.ParentCompanyId)

--display the data...
SELECT Aggregations.ParentCompanyId,
       Aggregations.Name,
       Aggregations.TotalSalesAmount,
       Aggregations.hierarchyDisplay
FROM Aggregations
ORDER BY Aggregations.hierarchy;
END;
```

Now, you can execute this procedure and see the sales by company, by region, and by the overall company, so executing

```
EXECUTE SqlGraph.Company$ReportSales 'Company HQ';
```

returns

```
ParentCompanyId hierarchyDisplay                      TotalSalesAmount
--------------- ------------------------------------- ------------------
1               Company HQ                            81.25
2                   --> Maine HQ                      51.25
7                   --> --> Portland Branch           22.50
8                   --> --> Camden Branch             28.75
```

```
3                  --> Tennessee HQ              30.00
4                  --> --> Nashville Branch       3.75
5                  --> --> Knoxville Branch      10.00
6                  --> --> Memphis Branch        16.25
```

Let's break this code down to look at how it works, as this technique can be really useful when working with tree structures. First is the expanded hierarchy. The first part of this is every node in the tree, related to itself:

```
--output the Expanded Hierarchy...
WITH ExpandedHierarchy (ParentCompanyId, ChildCompanyId)
AS (
    --gets all of the nodes of the hierarchy
    SELECT Company.CompanyId AS ParentCompanyId,
           Company.CompanyId AS ChildCompanyId
    FROM SqlGraph.Company
  )
SELECT *
FROM   ExpandedHierarchy
ORDER BY ExpandedHierarchy.ParentCompanyId;
```

Executing this query returns

```
ParentCompanyId ChildCompanyId
--------------- --------------
1               1
2               2
3               3
4               4
5               5
6               6
7               7
8               8
```

It is needed because for the MATCH clause to return these rows, there needs to be a cyclic relationship to the same node.

Next, the second half of the expanded hierarchy query uses a recursive relationship, although it only really does one iteration. Every node in the ExpandedHierarchy is expanded in the second half of the query:

```
WITH ExpandedHierarchy (ParentCompanyId, ChildCompanyId)
AS (
    --gets all of the nodes of the hierarchy
    SELECT Company.CompanyId AS ParentCompanyId,
           Company.CompanyId AS ChildCompanyId
    FROM SqlGraph.Company

    UNION ALL

    SELECT ExpandedHierarchy.ParentCompanyId,
           ToCompany.CompanyId
    FROM ExpandedHierarchy,
         SqlGraph.Company AS FromCompany,
         SqlGraph.ReportsTo,
         SqlGraph.Company AS ToCompany
    WHERE ExpandedHierarchy.ChildCompanyId = FromCompany.CompanyId
        AND MATCH(FromCompany-(ReportsTo)->ToCompany)
)
SELECT *
FROM    ExpandedHierarchy
--don't return the rows from the first query JUST for this
--example explanation only
WHERE ExpandedHierarchy.ParentCompanyId <> ExpandedHierarchy.ChildCompanyId
ORDER BY ParentCompanyId;
```

This returns

```
ParentCompanyId ChildCompanyId
--------------- --------------
1               2
1               3
1               4
1               5
1               6
1               7
1               8
2               7
2               8
3               4
3               5
3               6
```

You can see that 1 relates to every other node, then 2 and 3 (Tennessee and Maine) relate to their child rows. So now, combining the two sets' outputs, every row is related to itself and its child rows.

The rest of the query is fairly straightforward. The FilterAndSweeten CTE just joins the ExpandedHierarchy and filters only on parent rows that are output from the company name you passed in to Company$ReturnHierarchy. It handles filtering along with adding the data that will be output.

```
FilterAndSweeten AS
(
    SELECT ExpandedHierarchy.*,
            CompanyHierarchyDisplay.Hierarchy,
                CompanyHierarchyDisplay.HierarchyDisplay

    FROM  ExpandedHierarchy
    JOIN  [SqlGraph].[Company$ReturnHierarchy]
            (@DisplayFromNodeName) AS CompanyHierarchyDisplay
        ON CompanyHierarchyDisplay.CompanyId =
                    ExpandedHierarchy.ParentCompanyId
)
```

The CompanyTotals CTE just takes the sales data for each individual company and sums it:

```
,--get totals for each Company for the aggregate
    CompanyTotals
AS (SELECT CompanyId,
           SUM(cast(Amount as decimal(20,2))) AS TotalAmount
   FROM SqlGraph.Sale
   GROUP BY CompanyId),
--aggregate each Company for the Company
```

Then you aggregate the data to the ParentCompany values, including the stuff you need for the final display:

```
Aggregations AS
(SELECT FilterAndSweeten.ParentCompanyId,
        SUM(CompanyTotals.TotalAmount) AS TotalSalesAmount,
        MAX(hierarchy) AS hierarchy,
        MAX(hierarchyDisplay) AS hierarchyDisplay
  FROM FilterAndSweeten
     JOIN CompanyTotals
        ON CompanyTotals.CompanyId =
                      FilterAndSweeten.ChildCompanyId
  GROUP BY FilterAndSweeten.ParentCompanyId)
```

Finally, the data is displayed in this extra step to just to make the sorting easier:

```
--display the data...
SELECT Aggregations.ParentCompanyId,
      Aggregations.hierarchyDisplay,
      Aggregations.TotalSalesAmount
FROM Aggregations
ORDER BY Aggregations.hierarchy
END;
```

Obviously, there is a lot going on in the code, but like most SQL code, it is quite straightforward once you dig into what it is doing, and it uses the relational engine and graph engine in very powerful ways.

Summary

In this chapter, I presented much of the code you will need to implement your own tree structures for your organization: methods to create, modify, query, and even destroy a hierarchy.

So far, you have used a very small dataset, but in the next chapter, you will increase the amount of data by five orders of magnitude and explore methods of building your own even larger datasets (assuming you have more than eight nodes in your production trees).

CHAPTER 6

Tree Structures, Algorithms, and Performance

One of the most universally useful versions of a graph we have discussed (especially in Chapter 5) is a tree. It shows up in sales organizations where regions roll up to districts, which in turn roll up to sites and then to individual salespersons. Rolling up and comparing sales at each level year over year is one of the most important reports many organizations have. Rolling up sales by region is also be one of my primary demonstrations for each of the tree implementations I include in the individual chapters that will cover these methods in greater detail.

So far I haven't talked too much about how much data you can process using the SQL Graph objects. In this chapter, you are going to be putting not only the SQL Graph objects to test, but you are also going to learn a couple of other ways you can create tree objects in SQL Server and get some insight into how they perform.

For the data structure configurations (other than SQL Graph, which was introduced in Chapter 5), you will see the basic algorithm for how the method works, the code to insert data, and how to replicate the queries on the data as built in Chapter 5 for SQL Graph. (The download contains the entire implementation details to match the SQL Graph objects created in the previous chapter, as well as several other implementations.)

After exploring the algorithms, you will use some test data scripts to load varying sized data samples and then you will compare how SQL Graph compares to the other algorithms, both in querying lots of rows as well as creating a lot of rows.

© Louis Davidson 2023
L. Davidson, *Practical Graph Structures in SQL Server and Azure SQL*,
https://doi.org/10.1007/978-1-4842-9459-8_6

Alternative Tree Implementation

All the graphs we have discussed so far have been variations on the adjacency list theme. We have a table to hold the relationships (edge) between two objects (nodes) and, depending on the limitations we put on the relationship key values, we get a cyclic or acyclic graph. For pretty much any graph configuration other than a strict tree structure, this is an optimum implementation.

Using an adjacency list/breadth-first algorithm in relational tables (and even graph structures) can have some performance limitations (each level you must fetch adds costs, and for really large trees it can add up pretty quickly due to the storage costs). Some uses of trees need extremely low latency access (for example, when you log into a computer system, you are probably in multiple security groups that are also members of security groups, and you don't want users waiting even seconds to get their security fetched). As such, you will learn a couple of performance-friendly methods to increase certain kinds of performance (at slightly higher maintenance costs, since magic truly does come at a price).

Luckily, trees are very specific structures that are rigid compared to other graph uses. To help with the performance issues, some very enterprising people defined several methods of implementing a tree in a relational database using other methods than the adjacency list method we have discussed in this book so far.

In this chapter, you will use the exact same tree structure as in Chapter 5, which you can see in Figure 6-1 (this is the same graph as Chapter 5's Figure 5-1). Keeping a steady output from your queries is essential when comparing algorithms, both for performance and applicability to your solution. Later in this chapter, I will introduce five fixed sets of data that I will use for the performance tests, and a big part of refining these algorithms was to make sure they all output the same answers when asked the same questions.

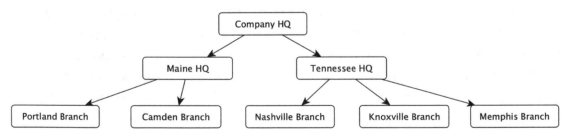

Figure 6-1. *Example tree structure*

Those five sets of data, randomly generated, will help gauge the time to load a tree and process a tree. By "process a tree," you will build code that tests common processes you will do with a tree (using the objects introduced in Chapter 5), such as summarizing the data for each node in the tree. Each root node will be assigned some amount of sales data, and then you will present the output of the amount of sales at each branch, local headquarters, and company headquarters. Each of the methods of implementing a tree will do this differently.

I have so far talked about the adjacency list, and I include the structure as it could be built in Figure 6-2. You know that the internals of the SQL Graph data structures used so far are similar to this, where there is a separate table that stores the Company and ReportsTo Company.

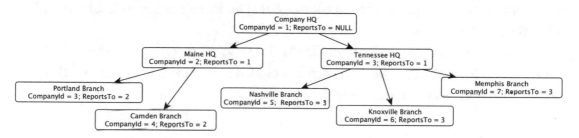

Figure 6-2. *Adjacency list example*

In this chapter, you will learn about two additional methods of storing your graph data in permanent tables, which have some advantage over, or assistance with, the SQL Graph/adjacency list method.

- **Path technique:** Instead of storing adjacent members in the graph, you store the path from the node to the tree root in a formatted text string. This is a very-simple-to-query, moderately-hard-to-maintain method that provides amazing performance.

- **Adding helper tables:** Adding tables that serve as indexes in the structure and precalculating data to allow queriers to skip some of the iterative operations that are required when processing tree.

There are a few other methods I want to briefly mention but I won't fully implement for this book. The first is using the hierarchyid datatype in SQL Server. While not terrible, SQL Graph is a better implementation overall and ought to be the way you go when working with graphs.

The second is really interesting, but the pain is worse than the value for almost any implementations I can think of. This is the nested sets, but the limitations and costs led me to leave it out of the book. There were two limiting factors for me. One is that loading a nested set structure is time-consuming row by row. The performance benefits over some other methods are painful. The other is that viewing the data is a hierarchical view isn't natural to the method. It is, however, extremely efficient at finding the children and parents of a row in a graph of any size.

Nested sets were introduced in 1992 by Michael J. Kamfonas in an article titled "Recursive Hierarchies: The Relational Taboo!" in *The Relational Journal*, October/November 1992. It is also a favorite method of Joe Celko, who has written a book about hierarchies in *Joe Celko's Trees and Hierarchies in SQL for Smarties* (Morgan Kaufmann, 2004); check it out (now in its second edition, 2012) for further reading about this and other types of hierarchies.

(Note: In my drsqlgithub repository in the GraphBook1 project, there is bonus code that implements far more than what is included in the book. It is on my GitHub repository because it will continue to grow as time passes.)

Path Technique

The path technique takes a textual path representation and stores it to make accessing data quick. Figure 6-3 shows the sample graph with the path values.

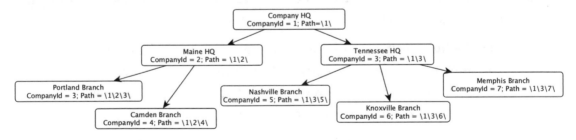

Figure 6-3. *Sample graph structure with path indicated*

I don't really know who originated this method, but I learned it from Paul Nielsen many years ago when we were chatting about the nested sets method I had only recently heard of. His point was about how easy and fast this method is. It really and truly is. Once you store the data, you have this easy-to-query structure that can be interrogated with straightforward SQL queries with no looping needed.

The base of this method is storing every node's path from root to that node. With that information, querying for children or parent nodes is as simple as using a LIKE expression. Typically, each of the path tags in the hierarchy will use the surrogate key for the key values in the path. All that really matters is that it is a relatively immutable value (because changing the key value requires changing other rows that use it in the path value) and that it is small (this isn't 100% necessary, but the longer the values, the fewer values can fit in the string and still be indexable). SQL Server 2016 and later have a limitation of 1700 bytes in a non-clustered index, which is a pretty deep tree since an integer will always fit in 10 characters.

Looking back at Figure 6-3, the path for the Knoxville Branch row is \1\3\6\. The CompanyId is 6, which gives you the current node's value. Then 3 is the next parent, and 1 is the root parent.

With the path formed and stored in this manner, you can find all the children of a node using the path in simple LIKE expression. For example, to get the children of the Maine HQ node, you can use a WHERE clause such as WHERE Path LIKE '\1\2\%' to get the children or LIKE '\1\2[^0-9]%' if you don't wish to include the trailing delimiter in your path values. The [^ makes sure the following character after your string is not a number and the path to the parents is directly in the path too. So, the parents of the Portland Branch, whose path is '\1\2\4\', are '\1\2\' and '\1\'. Using STRING_SPLIT(PathValue,'\') in SQL Server 2016 and later, this is a fairly easy, and more importantly, non-iterative process as well to get the parent nodes in a fairly simple query.

One of the great things about the path method is that it readily uses indexes for most of your queries, because most times it will use the left side of a string and/or the values from the primary key of the actual row. Even when you query the structure, you can get a view (ordered by surrogate key values) of the data in a hierarchical fashion quite easily. Your code can also be adjusted to include a user-readable hierarchy for ordering the output, and that path can be far larger since you ideally would not be searching on that data.

Bear in mind that you can index really deep paths, since in 1700 bytes you can generally achieve a max of around 150-170 levels, knowing any integer fits into 10 characters and there will be a separator. However, once your paths are in this range of length, you could only end up with four keys per page, which is not going to give amazing performance in any case.

Maintaining the structures using the path method is somewhat of a downside in comparison to using an adjacency list type method. Any change to the parent of a node can mean modifying the children of that row as well, since they will carry around your node's path, too. This is referred to as **reparenting** when working with a tree. If your path is \1\2\3\4\, and node with a key value of 2 is reparented to be under 6, 2's path needs to change to \1\6\2\, and every child of 2 as well, which in certain cases could be hundreds or even millions of rows.

It can generally be done with using the REPLACE function, but the biggest issue isn't how hard the algorithm is to code but how it will affect performance. The more rows you must modify, the more rows need to be locked, since you will want to do modifications to your tree structures in an explicit transaction in case there is an error.

Probably the biggest concern with this method is that the data does not protect itself very well. With the adjacency list model of SQL Graph, the main concern you have with keeping the structure a proper tree is making sure that every node is in a relationship, in some way, to the root node. But the path is just a string, and there is no easy way to make sure that you don't update the path to be 'fred' or '10000', or worse yet '\1\2\30000\432\', and there aren't nodes with a key of 30000 or 2. At that point you might be in a world of hurt if you have millions of rows.

For a reparent or even a delete, what happens to child rows is important. You can't delete path '\1\2\3\' without deleting or reparenting '\1\2\3\4\' or you will leave this orphaned row in the structure and unlike a tree, where a parentless node will become a root node by default, using the path method, it will just become invalid because not every referenced node in the path exists.

Code

In this section, you are going to see the code that shows how the insert is done with the path method. First up is the table structure. Note that the CompanyId column is not a column with the identity property. Because the path will use the CompanyId values, generating the value with a SEQUENCE object is far easier. As usual, I will comment the code so it is hopefully clear what it is doing.

Table Create Script

The create script is quite easy, just the surrogate key, an identifier, and the path (which I make the max size a non-clustered index can hold). This code is in the Chapter 6 downloads as 1300-Path Method-Objects.sql.

```
CREATE SCHEMA PathMethod;

CREATE TABLE PathMethod.Company
(
    CompanyId INT  NOT NULL CONSTRAINT PKCompany PRIMARY KEY,
    Name VARCHAR(20)  NOT NULL CONSTRAINT AKCompany_Name UNIQUE,
    Path VARCHAR(1700) NOT NULL INDEX Path
);
--indexes max out at 1700 bytes. Allows for at least a 1600+
--deep Hierarchy, which is very deep for most uses, but is a
--limitation. Removing the index could really hurt perf.
```

Insert New Rows

For the insert, basically the path of the node is acquired for the parent node and then used as the prefix for the new node in the data structure:

```
CREATE PROCEDURE PathMethod.Company$Insert
    @Name                 varchar(20),
    @ParentCompanyName varchar(20)
AS
BEGIN
    --gets Path, which looks like \CompanyId\CompanyId\...
    DECLARE @ParentPath varchar(1700) =
                        COALESCE(( SELECT Company.Path
                                   FROM   PathMethod.Company
                                   WHERE  Company.Name =
                                     @ParentCompanyName), '\');
    --used a SEQUENCE instead of identity because it made it
    --easier to be able to do the next step in a single statement
    --since the surrogate key is part of the value in the path
```

```
--you could do this with an insert using SCOPE_IDENTITY(),
--and then update the path if you would rather

DECLARE @NewCompanyId int = NEXT VALUE FOR
                                    PathMethod.Company_SEQUENCE;

--appends the new id to the parents Path
INSERT INTO PathMethod.Company(CompanyId, Name, Path)
SELECT @NewCompanyId, @Name,
        @ParentPath + CAST(@NewCompanyId AS varchar(10)) + '\';
END;
```

The download contains the sequence object and the procedure PathMetho. Sale$InsertTestData to load the sample values, just as in Chapter 5.

Return Hierarchy

Returning the hierarchy with the path method is more or less just a matter of formatting the output since the path is already stored:

```
CREATE OR ALTER FUNCTION PathMethod.Company$ReturnHierarchy
    @CompanyName varchar(20)
RETURNS @Output TABLE (CompanyId int Name varchar(20),
                        Level int, Hierarchy nvarchar(4000),
                        IdHierarchy nvarchar(4000),
                        HierarchyDisplay nvarchar(4000))
AS
BEGIN

DECLARE @CompanyId int,
            @CompanyPath varchar(12),
            @CompanyPathReplace varchar(12)

--get the CompanyId and path for the item you want
--to get the child rows of
SELECT @CompanyId = CompanyId,
        @CompanyPath = CONCAT('\',CompanyId,'\'),
        @CompanyPathReplace = Path --used for formatting
                                    --output without prefix
```

```
FROM    PathMethod.Company
WHERE   Name = @CompanyName;

WITH BaseRows AS
(
--get the child rows using the simple like expression
--to get child rows whose path startw with the parent
SELECT CompanyId, Name,
        --make the path look like it starts at searched node
        REPLACE(path,@CompanyPathReplace,@CompanyPath)
                                    AS IdHierarchy
FROM    PathMethod.Company
WHERE   Path LIKE @CompanyPathReplace + '%'
)
--output the rows
INSERT INTO @Output
(
    CompanyId,
    Name,
    Level,
    Hierarchy,
    IdHierarchy,
    hierarchyDisplay
)
SELECT Baserows.CompanyId, BaseRows.Name,
    LEN(IdHierarchy)
    - LEN(REPLACE(BaseRows.IdHierarchy,'\',''))-1 AS Level,
    'Not feasible', --This can be done with a replace,
                    --create this in your insert if essential
    BaseRows.IdHierarchy,
    --put in the arrows for the simple output
      REPLICATE('--> ',LEN(IdHierarchy) -
          LEN(REPLACE(BaseRows.IdHierarchy,'\',''))-2) + Name
                                    AS HieararchyDisplay
FROM BaseRows;

RETURN;
END;
```

Check For Child

Checking to see if a node is a child of another is a very clean process. You simply have to look to see where the two items are located in the same path. So, to see if company 1 is the parent to company 5, you simply need to find the row that looks like either '%\1\5%' or '%\1\%\5\%'. What is kind of cool is that you can decide if it is a child with just the two path values because the parent's path will a part of any child row's path.

```
CREATE OR ALTER FUNCTION PathMethod.Company$CheckForChild
(
    @CompanyName varchar(20),
    @CheckForChildOfCompanyName varchar(20)
)
RETURNS Bit
AS
BEGIN
    DECLARE @output bit = 0;

    --get the companyId of the item passed in
    DECLARE @CompanyPath varchar(1700)
    SELECT  @CompanyPath = Path
    FROM    PathMethod.Company
    WHERE   Name = @CompanyName;

    --get the company id for the child
    DECLARE @CheckForChildOfCompanyPath varchar(1700)
    SELECT  @CheckForChildOfCompanyPath = Path
    FROM    PathMethod.Company
    WHERE   Name = @CheckForChildOfCompanyName;

    --IF the item IS A child OF the company TO check, the
    --path will include parent company. No need to go back to
    --the table.
    IF REPLACE(@CompanyPath,@CheckForChildOfCompanyPath, '') <>
                                                @CompanyPath

      SET @output = 1;

      RETURN @output;
END;
```

Report Sales

Finally, the aggregation object. This works just like the SQL Graph example with a few important differences that will be covered in the code.

```
CREATE OR ALTER  PROCEDURE [PathMethod].[Company$ReportSales]
(
    @DisplayFromNodeName varchar(20)
)
AS
BEGIN

 --take the expanded Hierarchy...
 WITH ExpandedHierarchy
   AS (SELECT Company.CompanyId AS ParentCompanyId,
              ChildRows.CompanyId AS ChildCompanyId
       --join the table to itself finding rows that match
       --the path with the wildcard in a LIKE
       FROM   PathMethod.Company
              JOIN PathMethod.Company AS ChildRows
                  --note that this being % means the row will
                  --match itself in the join.
                  ON ChildRows.Path LIKE Company.Path + '%'
    ),

    --add in the formatting code and filter
    FilterAndSweeten AS (

    SELECT ExpandedHierarchy.*,
           CompanyHierarchyDisplay.IdHierarchy,
           CompanyHierarchyDisplay.HierarchyDisplay
    FROM   ExpandedHierarchy
              --The return hierarchy function gives us the
              --companyId to join with
              JOIN  PathMethod.[Company$ReturnHierarchy]
                (@DisplayFromNodeName) AS CompanyHierarchyDisplay
```

```
            ON CompanyHierarchyDisplay.CompanyId =
                            ExpandedHierarchy.ParentCompanyId
    )
    ,
    --get totals for each Company for the aggregate
    CompanyTotals AS
     (
            SELECT CompanyId, SUM(Amount) AS TotalAmount
            FROM    PathMethod.Sale
            GROUP BY CompanyId
    ),
    --aggregate each Company for the Company
    Aggregations AS (
    SELECT FilterAndSweeten.ParentCompanyId,
            SUM(CompanyTotals.TotalAmount) AS TotalSalesAmount,
            MAX(FilterAndSweeten.IdHierarchy) AS IdHiearchy,
            MAX(FilterAndSweeten.HierarchyDisplay)
                                        AS HiearachyDisplay

    FROM    FilterAndSweeten
                LEFT JOIN CompanyTotals
                    ON CompanyTotals.CompanyId =
                                FilterAndSweeten.ChildCompanyId
    GROUP  BY FilterAndSweeten.ParentCompanyId)

    --display the data...
    SELECT Company.CompanyId, Company.Name,
            Aggregations.TotalSalesAmount,
            Aggregations.HiearachyDisplay
    FROM    PathMethod.Company
             JOIN Aggregations
               ON Company.CompanyID = Aggregations.ParentCompanyID
    ORDER BY Aggregations.IdHiearchy

END;
```

The main difference in this code and the SQL Graph method in Chapter 5 is this block:

```
--join the table to itself finding rows that match
--the path with the wildcard in a LIKE
FROM    PathMethod.Company
        JOIN PathMethod.Company AS ChildRows
            --note that this being % means the row will
            --match itself in the join.
            ON ChildRows.Path LIKE Company.Path + '%'
```

This is quite cool in that you join the first set of rows (every row in the table) and join it with itself on the pattern.

Note   In the Chapter 6 file named `1301-PathMethod-Extended.sql`, I implement reparent and delete procedures.

Helper Table

One of the things that the techniques discussed so far (using SQL Graph, paths, and nested sets) all have in common is that when you use them, you are often processing rows in an iterative way or doing non-equality-based comparisons. This can sometimes be costly to process, especially for very large datasets. In this section, you are going to explore a couple of helper tables that can help to optimize the processes, especially when the data sets get really large and you can allow some amount of latency in your data processing.

To be fair, the gist of these techniques is something I often complain about in my writing and family gatherings (not that anyone listens over the turkey and dressing), and that is **denormalization**. The idea is that some of the things we have calculated on the fly so far, we persist, precalculated.

The main thing to understand is that like any denormalization that involves duplication of data, when the underlying data changes, you also must make sure the copies of the data matches that set to get proper answers to your queries. In my examples, I assume that you can rebuild your data set offline and do a complete rebuild of these copy tables. (In some cases, it may be advantageous to make your refreshes more targeted.)

This refresh process can make concurrent execution difficult, so a lot will depend on how often your data is modified and what performance issues you run into with your actual usage. It's not hard to adapt the following code to save the data in a staging table and merge it with the live table if desired.

I will demonstrate building two such tables:

Kimball helper table: This table takes the concept of the expanded hierarchy and instantiates it in a table. This obviously makes aggregation faster, but it also assists with other processes (and is a lot more obvious to a novice SQL programmer). As mentioned earlier in this chapter, this method is named for Ralph Kimball, who did a lot of great things for the data warehousing community for years.

Hierarchy display helper: In the FilterAndSweeten CTEs you built as part of the sales summary code, you used a function to fetch the data. This table you will be creating will prebuild that display table. In many ways, all you are doing is replicating the path method table from the adjacency list, letting you manage your hierarchies using the simpler SQL Graph tables, and then producing a table that is easier to work with when querying, especially if you do any reporting from these objects.

Kimball Helper Table

This method is going to be relatively simple to implement because you already more or less created the code earlier. The method is designed for dealing with hierarchies in reporting systems that deal with a lot of data, in a data warehousing/read-intensive setting. Even though it is designed for static data (typically refreshed daily), it can be useful in an OLTP setting if the hierarchy does not change frequently and there isn't a lot of contention with the physical resources of the table.

Going back to the adjacency list implementation, a subgraph of the adjacency list implementation is shown in Figure 6-4.

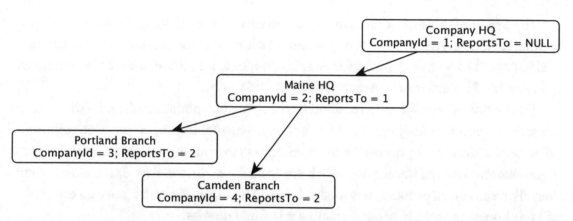

Figure 6-4. *Subgraph for example with values for the adjacency list technique repeated for the Kimball helper table method*

To implement this method, you will use a table of data that describes the hierarchy with one row per parent-to-child relationship for every level of the hierarchy. So, there is a row for Company HQ to Maine HQ, Company HQ to Portland Branch, and Maine HQ to Portland Branch and even one for each node, like Portland Branch to Portland Branch and Company HQ to CompanyHQ. The helper table provides the details about distance from parent to child, as well as any other useful information like if it is a root node or a leaf node. So, for the leftmost four items (1, 2, 4, 5) in the tree, you get rows like the following table:

ParentId	ChildId	Distance	RootNodeFlag	LeafRowFlag
1	1	0	1	0
1	2	1	0	0
1	3	2	0	0
1	3	2	0	0
2	2	0	0	0
2	3	1	0	1
2	4	1	0	1
3	3	0	0	1
4	4	0	0	1

The power of this technique is that now you can simply ask for all children of 1 by looking for WHERE ParentId = 1, or you can look for direct descendants of 2 by saying WHERE ParentId = 2 and Distance = 1. You can look for all leaf notes of the parent by querying WHERE ParentId = 1 and ChildLeafNode = 1.

The obvious downfall of this method is that it must be maintained, and if the structure is modified frequently, it could not be a reasonable general-purpose solution. To be honest, Kimball's purpose for the method was to optimize relational usage of hierarchies in the data warehouse, which are typically maintained by ETL and refreshed daily. For this sort of purpose, this method should be the quickest, because all queries will be almost completely based on simple relational queries.

Of all the methods, this one should be the most natural for users. I have known of companies that used just such a solution for corporate hierarchies, for example for row-level security, since that data changes very rarely and latency for the users is of utmost importance. (This discussion of the Kimball method is borrowed from my *Pro SQL Server 2012 Relational Database Design and Implementation* book (Apress, 2012).)

Note   You could extend this method to any graph structure, even a cyclic graph, but it would get very large and complex really fast. However, depending on the size and utilization of the structures, it may still be of value.

Code

This section contains the code that can be used for using the Kimball helper table.

Table Create Script

The table mirrors the structure introduced in the earlier examples:

```
--this table gives us the expanded hierarchy we used earlier to
--make aggregation and lookup easier
CREATE SCHEMA Helper;
GO
CREATE TABLE Helper.CompanyHierarchyHelper
(
    ParentCompanyId     int,
    ChildCompanyId      int,
```

```
    Distance              int,
    ParentRootNodeFlag bit
        CONSTRAINT DFLTCompanyHierarchyHelper_ParentRootNodeFlag
                                                DEFAULT 0,
    ChildLeafNodeFlag  bit
        CONSTRAINT DFLTCompanyHierarchyHelper_ChildLeafNodeFlag
                                                DEFAULT 0,
    --The primary key is from parent to child.
    CONSTRAINT PKCompanyHierarchyHelper PRIMARY KEY(
        ParentCompanyId,
        ChildCompanyId),
    --this index assists when looking for parent rows.
    INDEX ChlldToParent UNIQUE (
        ChildCompanyId,
        ParentCompanyId
        ),
);
```

Note that the primary key is on the ParentCompanyId and ChildCompanyId. You don't want the same combination to show up more than once. The following piece of code is used to maintain the data:

```
CREATE OR ALTER PROCEDURE Helper.CompanyHierarchyHelper$Rebuild
AS
 BEGIN
  SET NOCOUNT ON;
  --delete all the data in the fastest way possible
  TRUNCATE TABLE Helper.CompanyHierarchyHelper;

  WITH ExpandedHierarchy (ParentCompanyId,
                          ChildCompanyId, Distance)
  AS (
   --gets all of the nodes of the hierarchy because the
   --MATCH doesnt include the self relationship
```

```
    SELECT Company.CompanyId AS ParentCompanyId,
            Company.CompanyId AS ChildCompanyId,
            0 as Distance
    FROM SqlGraph.Company

    UNION ALL --Not recursive. Just need both sets

    --get the parent and child rows, along with the distance
    --from the root
    SELECT FromCompany.CompanyId AS ParentCompanyId,
            LAST_VALUE(ToCompany.CompanyId)
                        WITHIN GROUP (GRAPH PATH) ,
            COUNT(ToCompany.Name)
                        WITHIN GROUP (GRAPH PATH) AS Distance
      FROM SqlGraph.Company AS FromCompany,
           SqlGraph.ReportsTo FOR PATH as ReportsTo,
           SqlGraph.Company FOR PATH AS ToCompany
      WHERE MATCH(SHORTEST_PATH(FromCompany(-(ReportsTo)
                                                ->ToCompany)+))
)
INSERT INTO  Helper.CompanyHierarchyHelper(ParentCompanyId,
                                    ChildCompanyId, Distance)
SELECT ParentCompanyId, ChildCompanyId, Distance
FROM    ExpandedHierarchy
OPTION (MAXDOP 1);

--set the special flags

--root nodes are never children
UPDATE  Helper.CompanyHierarchyHelper
SET     ParentRootNodeFlag = 1
WHERE   ParentCompanyId NOT IN (SELECT ChildCompanyId
                                FROM Helper.CompanyHierarchyHelper
                                WHERE   parentCompanyId <>
                                                ChildCompanyId)
--LEAF nodes are never parents
UPDATE  Helper.CompanyHierarchyHelper
SET     ChildLeafNodeFlag = 1
```

180

```
WHERE   ChildCompanyId NOT IN (SELECT ParentCompanyId
                               FROM Helper.CompanyHierarchyHelper
                               WHERE parentCompanyId <>
                                                 ChildCompanyId)
END;
GO
```

The user who needs to refresh the data will simply execute this object and the table will be emptied and reloaded. Make sure users are not concurrently querying the object while you are loading it.

Check For Child

One place where this helper table can be useful is when checking for a child. Once you have the two id values, you can simply see if there is a row that has the parent and child id values. For example, if you are doing a security system, unless you have constant user changes, you could use a helper table to make security checks very fast.

```
CREATE OR ALTER FUNCTION Helper.Company$CheckForChild
(
    @CompanyName varchar(20),
    @CheckForChildOfCompanyName varchar(20)
)
RETURNS bit
AS
BEGIN
    DECLARE @output BIT = 0,@CompanyId int,
            @CheckForChildOfCompanyId int

    --translate the child companyId from parameter
    SELECT  @CompanyId = CompanyId
    FROM    SQLGraph.Company
    WHERE   Company.Name = @CompanyName;

    --translate the potential parentId from parameter
    SELECT  @CheckForChildOfCompanyId = CompanyId
    FROM    SQLGraph.Company
    WHERE   Company.Name = @CheckForChildOfCompanyName;
```

```
    --look for a row with the corresponding id values.
    SELECT @Output = 1
    FROM   Helper.CompanyHierarchyHelper
    WHERE  ParentCompanyId = @CheckForChildOfCompanyId
      AND  ChildCompanyId = @CompanyId

    RETURN @OutPut

END;
```

Hierarchy Display Helper

In this chapter, when using the SQLGraph.Company$ReportSales object, you use the SqlGraph.CompanyHierarchyDisplay view to sweeten your dataset with textual data for output. In this section, you are simply going to take the data that is represented by that view and store it in a table.

Code

This helper table is just a duplicate of the structure that you would get executing a SELECT INTO query using the CompanyHierarchyDisplay view object implemented in Chapter 5 and adding a few indexes (true story).

Table Create Script

```
CREATE TABLE Helper.HierarchyDisplayHelper(
    --one row per company
    CompanyId int NOT NULL
        CONSTRAINT PKHerarchyDisplayHelper PRIMARY KEY,
    HierarchyDisplay varchar(8000) NULL,
    Level int NOT NULL,
    Name varchar(20) NOT NULL
        CONSTRAINT AKHierarchyDisplayHelper UNIQUE,
    Hierarchy varchar(8000) NOT NULL
) ON [PRIMARY]
GO
```

Now create the following procedure to load the data. You are basically just querying the view as is and inserting into the table. I did include an OPTION(MAXDOP 1) at the end, as there can be issues with parallelism and the SQL Graph objects and for larger sets it behaves better single threaded. (As of this writing, based on SQL Server 2022, it is generally better to just add that to your coded objects that work with larger amounts of data with SQL Graph tables, which you will in the next two chapters when working with large data sets.)

```
CREATE PROCEDURE Helper.HierarchyDisplayHelper$Rebuild
AS
BEGIN
    TRUNCATE TABLE [Helper].[HierarchyDisplayHelper];

    INSERT INTO Helper.HierarchyDisplayHelper
        (CompanyId, HierarchyDisplay, Level, Name, Hierarchy)
    SELECT CompanyId, HierarchyDisplay, Level, Name, Hierarchy
    FROM    SqlGraph.CompanyHierarchyDisplay
    OPTION(MAXDOP 1); --when queries get complex, it is often
                      --better to use single threaded processing
                      --with sql graph
END;
```

Using the Helper Objects

Finally, let's pull this together and use the helper tables in the Company$ReportSales stored procedure by replacing the expanded hierarchy and filtering and sweeting code with the freshly created tables.

Report Sales

```
CREATE OR ALTER PROCEDURE Helper.Company$ReportSales
    @DisplayFromNodeName varchar(20)
AS
BEGIN
SET NOCOUNT ON;
--fetch the hierarchy for the node you are looking for by name
--we will use this just like using the path method ojbect
```

```
DECLARE @NodeHierarchy varchar(8000) = (
                                SELECT Hierarchy
                                FROM Helper.HierarchyDisplayHelper
                                WHERE Name = @DisplayFromNodeName);

--expanded hierarchy is now a table
--as is the display version.
WITH FilterAndSweeten AS
(
     SELECT ExpandedHierarchy.*,
            HierarchyDisplayHelper.Hierarchy,
            HierarchyDisplayHelper.HierarchyDisplay
     FROM  Helper.CompanyHierarchyHelper AS ExpandedHierarchy
           JOIN Helper.HierarchyDisplayHelper
               ON ExpandedHierarchy.ParentCompanyId =
                                 HierarchyDisplayHelper.CompanyId

     --filters the search to start with the path we sent in
     --the stuff after + makes sure the filter gets everything
     --like the node we fetched, as long as it doesn't have a
     --following digit.
     WHERE  HierarchyDisplayHelper.Hierarchy
                         LIKE @NodeHierarchy + '[^0-9]%'
      --include the root of the query, not character.
      OR   HierarchyDisplayHelper.Hierarchy = @NodeHierarchy
)
,--get totals for each Company for the aggregate
  CompanyTotals
AS (SELECT CompanyId,
           SUM(CAST(Amount AS decimal(20,2))) AS TotalAmount
    FROM SqlGraph.Sale
    GROUP BY CompanyId),

   --aggregate each Company for the Company
   Aggregations AS
   (SELECT FilterAndSweeten.ParentCompanyId,
           SUM(CompanyTotals.TotalAmount) AS TotalSalesAmount,
```

```
            MAX(Hierarchy) AS hierarchy,
            MAX(HierarchyDisplay) AS HierarchyDisplay
    FROM FilterAndSweeten
        JOIN CompanyTotals
            ON CompanyTotals.CompanyId =
                         FilterAndSweeten.ChildCompanyId
    GROUP BY FilterAndSweeten.ParentCompanyId)

--display the data...
SELECT Aggregations.ParentCompanyId,
       Aggregations.hierarchyDisplay,
       Aggregations.TotalSalesAmount
FROM Aggregations
ORDER BY Aggregations.hierarchy;
END;
```

Now you can use the hierarchy using the follow code. First, you refresh your two objects. (In a real system, if you are using both, you probably would make another procedure to call both, but no real need for our purposes.)

```
EXEC Helper.HierarchyDisplayHelper$Rebuild;
EXEC Helper.CompanyHierarchyHelper$Rebuild;
```

After this finishes (clearly instantly with your small number of tables, but it will take minutes at times with the very large tables in the downloads), run

```
EXECUTE Helper.Company$ReportSales 'Company HQ';
```

And you will see the set that you probably have seen before:

```
ParentCompanyId hierarchyDisplay                 TotalSalesAmount
--------------- ------------------------------   --------------------
1               Company HQ                       81.25
2               --> Maine HQ                     51.25
8               --> --> Camden Branch            28.75
7               --> --> Portland Branch          22.50
3               --> Tennessee HQ                 30.00
5               --> --> Knoxville Branch         10.00
```

```
6                 --> --> Memphis Branch      16.25
4                 --> --> Nashville Branch    3.75
```

Of course, this data set is very small, but in the next section, you will put this to the test.

Performance Comparison

I haven't talked much about performance so far in the book, but here is where I want to put the SQL Graph design to the test, along with the Path method and the Helper table.

To do this, I have created five test datasets that I use to create data. These scripts use the same format we have worked with throughout the last two chapters. There is a `SqlGraph.SmallSet` object that replicates that working set as a small baseline. Each of the scripts creates data one row at a time and creates five sales rows for each leaf node. The five scripts create a decent set of rows to process for test purposes:

Name	Row Count
Small	8
Large	3400
Wide	55301
Deep	42101
Huge	298001

If you need even larger datasets, there are Data Generator Script Producer files in the downloads that you can tailor to how you want your dataset to look. You can tune approximately how many rows you want per level and how many levels. For example, the `WideSet` is set to give you 5 levels of hierarchy, but the `Deepset` is set to give you 15 levels but not be so large or deep it takes long to run the scripts.

I ran these scripts and tests on my local test machine, which is by no means a server class device and is a few years old in technology. (I bought it from Amazon. This is the title: *Intel NUC 9 NUC9i7QNX (Intel 6-Core i7-9750H, 64GB RAM, 2TB PCIe SSD,*

2 x Thunderbolt, WiFi 6, HDMI, Win 10 Pro) Ghost Skull Canyon Extreme Gaming Box Elite). But it is a hefty local test computer and all it is running is an RTM copy of SQL Server 2022.

The way I run the scripts for testing is via my TestRig file. Once I have the data loaded, I just choose the schema that holds the objects, and I run three tests:

1. Fetch all children into a temp table twice, once from the root and once from another node that is not the root.

2. Run three checks for child examples using fixed node names in one statement.

3. Run two Report Sales runs, one for the root node and the other for the same hard-coded node value as for the fetch all children.

So, for the performance numbers. The smaller sets were all generally very fast enough that there was no real difference. See Table 6-1.

Table 6-1. *Load Times for the Different Graph Tools*

Name	Row Count	SQL Graph	Path	Helper Tables*
Small	8	0.014	0.013	0.007
Large	3400	3.53	4.00	0.37
Wide	55301	51	48	7
Deep	42101	32	29	16
Huge	298001	227	222	523

* Helper table load time is just to load the two helper tables. The complete load time would include the SQL Graph load time also.

The most interesting part of this is the load times for the Helper objects. As they got very much larger, the amount of time went up quickly. Part of this has to do with needing to run the code single threaded from a single file.

The real question is how much value the helper table is when I use the SQL Graph method of processing the tree. These values are covered in Table 6-2.

Table 6-2. *Approximate Times in Seconds to Aggregate the Sales for the*
Nodes Twice

Aggregate Tree Times				
Name	**Row Count**	**SQL Graph**	**Path**	**Helper Table**
Small	8	0.016	0.003	0.18
Large	3400	0.375	0.143	0.109
Wide	55301	8.69	5.65	0.8
Deep	42101	9.31	3.2	0.7
Huge	298001	96.3	13.6	5.9

Looking at the processing times in Table 6-2, you can see something kind of
interesting. Firstly, taking the time to create the helper tables is very much worth it for
querying the structures for any sort of reporting application, especially as your data
size increases. The path method is faster, partially because one of the helper tables is
essentially structured like the path one.

Finally, in Table in 6-3, you can see that even outputting 298 thousand rows into
a temp table, formatted for view is not that large of a task using any of the methods,
especially considering the machine being used (I never used all the RAM that I allocated
SQL Server, so this is basically a CPU issue, and I am only using a single CPU due to the
MAXDOP = 1). The path method already contains some of the data formatted as I want it
for the processing, so it generally is faster.

Table 6-3. *Approximate Times to Fetch All of the*
Children of a Node Twice

Fetch All Children Times			
Name	**Row Count**	**SQL Graph**	**Path**
Small	8	0.032	< .000000
Large	3400	0.078	0.032
Wide	55301	1.21	0.34
Deep	42101	1.08	0.33
Huge	298001	8.92	2.9

The final test that I performed was the test to say if I have NodeX, and NodeY, is NodeX a child of NodeY.? For every one of these tests, the time that it took using every algorithm was negligible and often did not show up in six digits of accuracy. Hence, I did not output this as a table, but the takeaway is that when you are working with a specific slice of the data, each of the methods can be very fast no matter how large the data set.

Just like almost any query using a relational engine, if indexes can be used to limit the data processed, you can have loads of data and work fast. The same is true for SQL Graph queries. It is only when large amounts of data get involved that the times to process increase (and parallelism becomes an issue, at least until SQL Server 2022 RTM).

Summary

In this second chapter on tree structures, I hope I was able to give you a feeling about not only a few techniques you might consider using with your tree structures but also how large a dataset can be processed on even a very small computer that is by no means server class. I didn't even try to dig too deep into hardware utilization and bandwidth, so your mileage clearly may vary when you start to work with these tools in your real systems and with server class hardware.

Either way, a tree of nearly 300,000 nodes is not a small size at all (nor is it amazingly large either), and we were able to process all the rows rather quickly, both using the native SQL Graph capabilities and with the alternative path method and with building helper tables. While I will admit that taking nearly 5 minutes to build the helper tables seemed like a lot of time, it could be worth it depending on your needs, especially if you are using graphs for analysis purposes. And if you can pay the latency in regenerating the helper tables, they could be put in a staging table and then swapped out without any users really noticing.

CHAPTER 7

Other Directed Acyclic Graphs

In this chapter, I want to include a relatively brief example and discussion of directed acyclic graphs (DAG) that are not trees. Back in Chapter 1, I gave them the name of a polyhierarchy, rather than a hierarchy.

Unlike a tree, in the structure I want to talk about in this chapter, a node in a polyhiearchy can have as many to/parent relationships as you want and need. This will make validation and programming for the structures a bit more interesting because the built-in code SQL Server implements doesn't cover all the uses of the graph.

The Problem Set

When working with a DAG that is not a tree, much of the common processing will be a subset of the algorithms you use to process a tree. In every case, you start from some node in the structure and work your way down through the structure, often using the same SHORTEST_PATH code you used previously.

There is just one minor snafu with the way SHORTEST_PATH works. It only finds each node once. For trees, since every node can only have one parent node, you are always guaranteed that it will only be found once in the path. Hence, no problem.

But consider the graph in Figure 7-1.

© Louis Davidson 2023
L. Davidson, *Practical Graph Structures in SQL Server and Azure SQL*,
https://doi.org/10.1007/978-1-4842-9459-8_7

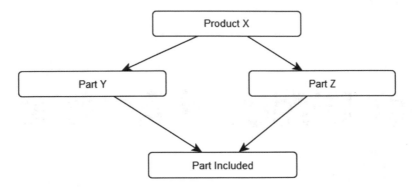

Figure 7-1. *Simple polyhierarchy*

If you use SHORTEST_PATH to see if Product X includes Part Included, it will show up as being related to either Part Y or Part Z, but not both. So, if you just want to know that Part Included is *somewhere* in Product X, SHORTEST_PATH works fine.

But often in a graph like this (commonly referred to as a bill of materials) you want to know all the places where that part is included and likely even how many of that part is included in the entire structure.

Consider next if the graph was actually like this one in Figure 7-2.

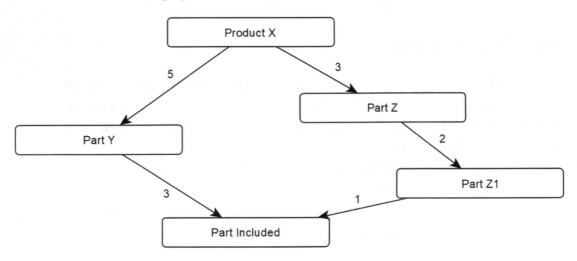

Figure 7-2. *Expanded bill of materials example group*

If you use SHORTEST_PATH on this graph to determine where you are using the Part Included, it will only show up as being part of Part Y, unless you start traversing from Part Z. When you start looking at the code to rectify this issue, this thought process kind of indicates what you must do to handle this in code. Traverse the tree one level at a time and get all nodes. Luckily, SQL offers the CTE construct that makes this relatively easy to do (though not in comparison to SHORTEST_PATH).

In a bill of materials, you also commonly will have magnitudes on the edges. Take a box of donuts. Say the box contains two Plain, three Chocolate Covered, and eight Crème Filled. If you are summing sales from the donut box structure, you have four nodes: one for the box and three adjacent nodes for each type of donut. The edges have magnitude. And every receipt is a node in the daily sales structure, where each receipt is independent but the products they include are the same.

As demonstrated in the past chapter, summing edge values in a tree is quite simple. Here, however, you run into the issues with SHORTEST_PATH. Values will be dropped off any aggregates as nodes show up in the structure more than one time. So if you try to sum the sales of all maple bacon donuts for the day via SHORTEST_PATH, you might see that only 12 were sold. (They were delicious.)

So, you need to change the approach to how you process the data somewhat and I will show that in this chapter.

The Example

For this chapter, you are going to implement a very simple bill of materials (shortened to BOM when it gets repetitive). This example is of a simple shelf system you might purchase from your favorite purveyor of meatballs (the reference is meaningless to the example, but if you know, you know).

What looks like a huge solid shelf is actually packaged in about 1,000 pieces. Some of those pieces are used in multiple areas of the shelves. It is very common for there to be repetition in the parts included, from screws and dowels to shelves and pieces of glass. Anything that can be reused from product to product is reused.

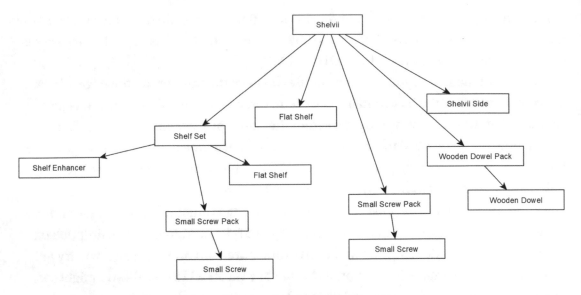

Figure 7-3. *Breakdown of the fictional Shelvii shelf system*

In Figure 7-3, I sketched a tree representation of what I call the Shelvii. Note that there are some duplications in the names found in the structure, as the Small Screw Pack and Small Screw nodes are in there more than one time. There are identifiers that are key values for the overall product system because things like the Wooden Dowel Pack probably show up in other products like the Tablii system, and there are probably various sized packs of dowels that can be included. This example is only as complex as I needed to show the basic issues. It would not be hard to extrapolate to multiple products, product lines, and so on.

There is also a Flat Shelf that is repeated for the main system. The idea is that the same flat shelf is used for the top and the bottom, but just doesn't need the shelf enhancer, so it is standalone. Note too that I completely ignore packaging in this discussion. Only the parts that make up the shelf are included, and I ignore details like if the part can be sold individually too.

Without turning this into a modular furniture design article, I wanted to include a reasonably realistic example because there are a few things you will almost certainly want to do with this data that is unlike a tree. In Figure 7-4, I remodeled this graph and consolidated the nodes that were the same into a DAG. In the first drawing, there were two Small Screw Pack nodes; there is now just one, but there are two relationships that connect to that one node.

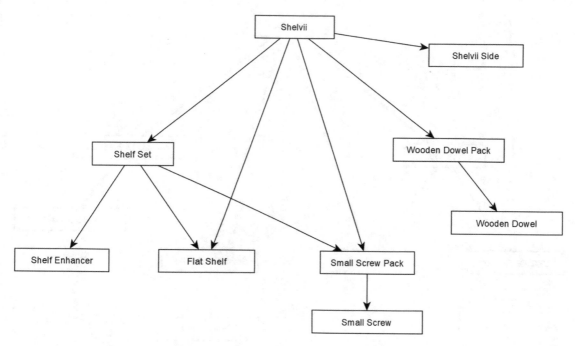

Figure 7-4. *DAG that represents reuse of items in structure*

Now the graph shows that both the Shelvii node and the Shelf Set node are parents to the Small Screw Pack nodes. This tells the person fetching these items to fetch (at least) two of the Small Screw Pack bags if they are assembling the entire product all at once.

I see processes to create packaging to match each of the nodes. So there are bins of Shelf Enhancers, Flat Shelves, Small Screws, Wooden Dowels, and Shelvii Sides. Proceed up the list, and there are processes to package a Shelf Set, Small Screw Pack, and Wooden Dowel Pack and still more bins to hold them. Some of these packs may be used in different shelf systems, some not. If one system needs 20 small screws and another 2, then there is more than one Small Screw Pack size. For sake of brevity, give me a modicum of leeway in my example to keep it simple.

Lastly, to finish up the setup, we need magnitudes. In Figure 7-5, I add the number of each item needed per shelf system.

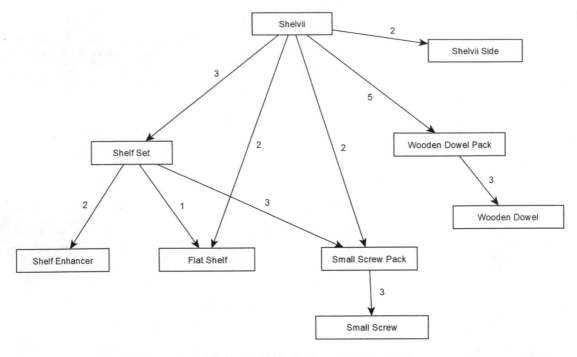

Figure 7-5. *Fleshed-out graph for the Shelvii project*

In the downloads for this chapter, I include the typical objects for this structure and queries to build the node and edge table. I keep it to just the necessary data needed to represent the DAG. There is a PartsSystem.Part node table (with a trigger that prevents cycles) and a PartsSystem.Includes edge. I also include an interface view so you can work with the data using simple INSERT, UPDATE, and DELETE statements.

The edge has an IncludeCount column. I also built a PartsSystem_UI schema that lets us insert new Parts relationships very easily (as covered back in Chapter 4). All of this code is in the downloads in the Chapter 7 file named 0001-CreateObjects.sql. The data is loaded using the 0002-LoadData.sql file.

This query shows the data in the system after executing the queries in the aforementioned files:

```
SELECT *
FROM   PartsSystem_UI.Part_Includes_Part;
```

This returns the following data (which matches Figure 7-5):

```
PartName                     IncludeCount IncludesPartName
----------------------- ------------ ----------------------------
Shelvii                       3          Shelf Set
Shelvii                       2          Flat Shelf
Shelvii                       5          Small Wooden Dowel Pack
Shelvii                       2          Shelvii Side
Shelvii                       2          Small Screw Pack
Shelf Set                     2          Shelvii Shelf Enhancer
Shelf Set                     1          Flat Shelf
Shelf Set                     3          Small Screw Pack
Small Screw Pack              3          Small Screw
Small Wooden Dowel Pack  3          Wooden Dowel
```

In the rest of the chapter, you will implement several of the types of queries you will typically want to do with a bill of materials:

- Determining if a part is used in a build

- Picking items for a certain build like the screws for the Screw Pack or shelves for the Shelf Set

- Printing and summing out the parts list for a build

Determining If a Part Is Used in a Build

This one of the tasks that is straightforward to do using a SHORTEST_PATH query. Since all you are trying to do is see what parts are used, you only need them to show up once in the list. So, you can do the following query that simply uses SHORTEST_PATH:

```
        --the item that is connected. Will be unique
SELECT LAST_VALUE(IncludesPart.PartName)
        WITHIN GROUP (GRAPH PATH) AS ConnectedItem,
        --show us the path that got us this connection
        STRING_AGG(IncludesPart.PartName, '->') WITHIN GROUP
                                        (GRAPH PATH) AS Path
FROM    PartsSystem.Part AS Part,
```

```
        PartsSystem.Includes FOR PATH AS Includes,
        PartsSystem.Part FOR PATH AS IncludesPart
WHERE   Part.PartName = 'Shelvii'
  AND    MATCH(SHORTEST_PATH(Part(-(Includes)->IncludesPart)+))
ORDER BY ConnectedItem;
```

I include it in the output to show which path was chosen for curiosity only. Realistically, you don't really need the path in this output because what you want are the parts that made up the Shelvii system.

```
ConnectedItem              Path
----------------------     -------------------------------------
Flat Shelf                 Flat Shelf
Shelf Set                  Shelf Set
Shelvii Shelf Enhancer     Shelf Set->Shelvii Shelf Enhancer
Shelvii Side               Shelvii Side
Small Screw                Small Screw Pack->Small Screw
Small Screw Pack           Small Screw Pack
Small Wooden Dowel Pack    Small Wooden Dowel Pack
Wooden Dowel               Small Wooden Dowel Pack->Wooden Dowel
```

One thing to note is that you have only sort of answered the question. This query provides you with the entire list, including containers. The Shelf Set is actually not a physical thing; it is a set of physical things that you must gather (plus a carton, but as previously noted, we're ignoring that in this example). Whether this matters is based on your point of view.

```
WITH BaseRows AS
(
SELECT LAST_VALUE(IncludesPart.PartName)
         WITHIN GROUP (GRAPH PATH) AS ConnectedItem,
       STRING_AGG(IncludesPart.PartName, '->')
         WITHIN GROUP (GRAPH PATH) AS Path,
       --capture the node_id so we can eliminate the non-leafs
       LAST_VALUE(IncludesPart.$node_id)
         WITHIN GROUP (GRAPH PATH) AS ConnectedItemNodeId
FROM   PartsSystem.Part AS Part,
       PartsSystem.Includes FOR PATH AS Includes,
```

```
        PartsSystem.Part FOR PATH AS IncludesPart
WHERE   Part.PartName = 'Shelvii'
    AND MATCH(SHORTEST_PATH(Part(-(Includes)->IncludesPart)+))
)
--filter rows where the node is parent in the structure
SELECT ConnectedItem, Path
FROM BaseRows
WHERE NOT EXISTS (SELECT *
                  FROM    PartsSystem.Includes
                  WHERE   $from_id = ConnectedItemNodeId)
ORDER BY ConnectedItem;
```

This now only returns

```
ConnectedItem              Path
----------------------     --------------------------------------
Flat Shelf                 Flat Shelf
Shelvii Shelf Enhancer     Shelf Set->Shelvii Shelf Enhancer
Shelvii Side               Shelvii Side
Small Screw                Small Screw Pack->Small Screw
Wooden Dowel               Small Wooden Dowel Pack->Wooden Dowel
```

Look back at Figure 7-5 and you will see that the leaf nodes do in fact show up in this query and this should represent the raw materials types you need to put together a Shelvii kit.

You can start the processing at any level in the object too. Start at the Shelf Set by changing the line to filter the Shelf Set instead of Shelvii:

```
WHERE   Part.PartName = 'Shelf Set':
```

Now you will see that it just has the three rows:

```
ConnectedItem        Path
-------------------  ---------------------------------
Flat Shelf           Flat Shelf
Shelf Enchancer      Shelf Enchancer
Small Screw          Small Screw Pack->Small Screw
```

Picking Items for a Build

Now let's go the other direction. You now don't care what makes up each part physically; you want to assemble or package a shelf. You are given some number of a given packages to build, and somewhere there is a picklist (which tells you what to go pick from the shelves).

The picklist query **should** be quite simple because you need only go one level down the tree to get the data to output. So, if you are grabbing the parts to put together a Shelvii, you just need to go fetch the parts (bundled or raw) that make it up:

```
SELECT IncludesPart.PartName, Includes.IncludeCount
FROM   PartsSystem.Part AS Part,
       PartsSystem.Includes AS Includes,
       PartsSystem.Part AS IncludesPart
WHERE  Part.PartName = 'Shelvii'
   AND MATCH(Part-(Includes)->IncludesPart);
```

This returns

```
PartName                    IncludeCount
----------------------      ------------
Shelf Set                   3
Flat Shelf                  2
Small Wooden Dowl Pack      5
Shelvii Side                2
Small Screw Pack            2
```

The idea of a build like this is that the Shelf Set and packs of fasteners are already packaged in another process (to streamline the packaging process). Obviously, this is tedious job, but it's faster than having to put together each package before assembling the entire package. If you have multiple orders that all need Small Screw Packs, ideally you make up that many Small Screw Packs. The you move on to Shelf Sets (which include the Small Screw Packs) and so on.

So, you take this list (with the bin locations and other bits of data you might need that I did not include for this chapter), go grab the pieces you need, and put them in the package you are building, just like someone did earlier with the Small Screw Pack:

```
SELECT IncludesPart.PartName, Includes.IncludeCount
FROM   PartsSystem.Part AS Part,
       PartsSystem.Includes AS Includes,
       PartsSystem.Part AS IncludesPart
WHERE  Part.PartName = 'Small Screw Pack'
   AND MATCH(Part-(Includes)->IncludesPart);
```

This returns the following:

```
PartName                        IncludeCount
------------------------------- ------------
Small Screw                     3
```

In the next section, you will use that `IncludeCount` column to determine how many screws it take to put together your entire shelf.

Printing Out the Parts List for a Build

Looking at the breakdown of all the parts that go into a product probably isn't needed too much by the assemblers, but it is very important for the people ordering future products. How many do we need? How and in what products are they used?

Here is where we get into trouble with the base syntax. `SHORTEST_PATH` fails us because it only gives us a single path from root (of the subgraph or graph) to the child. So, if you want to print out the list of things you need for the entire build, you are going to have to use a different method. To make your BOM query lossless, you need to basically go to each node and see what items they include, then see what their child rows include, until you are down to the base items (the leaf nodes).

The solution is to take control of the breadth-first search. To do this, you use a recursive CTE. On each level of the query, you simply use a `MATCH` expression to fetch the items that make up one build and then fetch the items that make up the next build, over and over. For example, to see all the parts that make up the Shelvii, where they go, and how many parts you need, you can use the following query. How the query works is documented in the code.

```
WITH BaseRows
AS (
    --the CTE anchor is just the starting node that
    --you want to see
```

```
    --the breakdown
    SELECT Part.$node_id AS PartNodeId,
            Part.$node_id  AS RelatedToPartNodeId,
            Part.PartName,
            1 AS IncludeCount,
         --the path that contains the readable path we have
          --built in all examples
            CAST('' AS NVARCHAR(4000)) AS Path,
            0 AS level --the level
    FROM PartsSystem.Part
    WHERE Part.Partname = 'Shelvii'
    UNION ALL
    --pretty typical 1 level graph query:
    SELECT Part.$node_id AS ItemId,
            IncludesPart.$node_id AS RelatedToItemId,
            IncludesPart.PartName,
            Includes.IncludeCount,
            BaseRows.Path + ' > ' + IncludesPart.PartName,
            BaseRows.level + 1
    FROM PartsSystem.Part,
        PartsSystem.Includes,
        PartsSystem.Part AS IncludesPart,
        BaseRows --this is what makes it recursive. Joining
                  --back the the set named BaseRows.
    WHERE MATCH(Part-(Includes)->IncludesPart)
      --this joins the anchor to the recursive part of the query
       AND BaseRows.RelatedToPartNodeId = Part.$node_id
     )
SELECT PartName, IncludeCount as IncCt, BaseRows.Path
FROM BaseRows
WHERE BaseRows.PartName <> 'Shelvii'
ORDER BY Path
GO
```

This returns the following, unaggregated results:

```
PartName                   IncCt Path
----------------------     ----- ------------------------------------
Flat Shelf                 2     > Flat Shelf
Shelf Set                  3     > Shelf Set
Flat Shelf                 1     > Shelf Set > Flat Shelf
Shelvii Shelf Enhancer     2     > Shelf Set > Shelvii Shelf ...
Small Screw Pack           3     > Shelf Set > Small Screw Pack
Small Screw                3     > Shelf Set > Small Screw Pac...
Shelvii Side               2     > Shelvii Side
Small Screw Pack           2     > Small Screw Pack
Small Screw                3     > Small Screw Pack > Small Screw
Small Wooden Dowel Pack    5     > Small Wooden Dowel Pack
Wooden Dowel               3     > Small Wooden Dowel Pack > ...
```

This gives you a breakdown of parts, what they are connected to, and the number at each level. You can see that Flat Shelf shows up a couple of times, so the next step is to aggregate the raw materials counts needed for your Shelvii. But while you **do** have three Small Screws in a pack, the number you need is actually based on the number per pack, along with the number in each edge along the way to the anchor row of the query.

Consider the subgraph displayed in Figure 7-6. Shelvii needs three Shelf Sets that use two Small Screw Packs, which in turn use three Small Screws. The Shelvii system itself use two packs directly. You need to calculate the entire IncludeCount to be not just be the count in a pack but to be the cumulative of all levels, and for that you use multiplication.

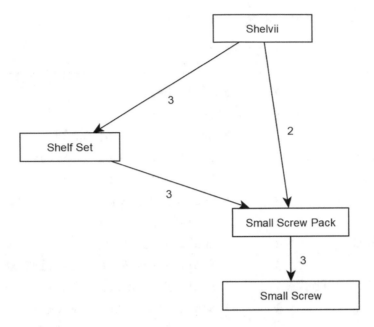

Figure 7-6. *Subgraph to show Small Screw Pack and Small Screw utilization*

To adjust the query used, in the recursive part of the CTE, instead of this line

```
Includes.IncludeCount,
```

change it to

```
BaseRows.IncludeCount * Includes.IncludeCount,
```

This changes the query so that at every level, it will multiple the number of items in each level with the next level. So, if you have 3 packs of 3 screws, you will be using (3 * 3) = 9 screws.

Now the output looks like this:

```
PartName                 IncCt Path
-----------------------  ----- -----------------------------------
Flat Shelf                 2    > Flat Shelf
Flat Shelf                 3    > Shelf Set > Flat Shelf
Shelf Set                  3    > Shelf Set
Shelvii Shelf Enhancer     6    > Shelf Set > Shelvii Shel...
Shelvii Side               2    > Shelvii Side
Small Screw                6    > Small Screw Pack > Small Screw
```

```
Small Screw                   27    > Shelf Set > Small Screw Pac...
Small Screw Pack              9     > Shelf Set > Small Screw Pack
Small Screw Pack              2     > Small Screw Pack
Small Wooden Dowel Pack       5     > Small Wooden Dowel Pack
Wooden Dowel                  15    > Small Wooden Dowel Pack > ...
```

Thinking of the shelves, you need two for the top and bottom and three for the inside shelves. You can see that in the output.

For the screws, you need (3 * 3 * 3) for the three Shelf Sets in Shelvii and (2 * 3) for the base Shelvii build, which you can see in the output is 27 and 6. Finally, you filter out the non-leaf nodes so the output makes sense to a reader.

```sql
WITH BaseRows
AS (
      --the CTE anchor is just the starting node that you want to
      --see --the breakdown
    SELECT Part.$node_id AS PartNodeId,
           Part.$node_id  AS RelatedToPartNodeId,
           Part.PartName,
           1 as IncludeCount,
        --the path that contains the readable path we have
        --built in all examples
           CAST('' AS NVARCHAR(4000)) AS Path,
           0 AS level --the level
    FROM PartsSystem.Part
    WHERE Part.Partname = 'Shelvii'
    UNION ALL
    --pretty typical 1 level graph query:
    SELECT Part.$node_id AS ItemId,
           IncludesPart.$node_id AS RelatedToPartNodeId,
           IncludesPart.PartName,
           BaseRows.IncludeCount * Includes.IncludeCount,
           BaseRows.Path + ' > ' + IncludesPart.PartName,
           BaseRows.level + 1
    FROM PartsSystem.Part,
         PartsSystem.Includes,
```

```
        PartsSystem.Part AS IncludesPart,
        BaseRows --this is what makes it recursive
    WHERE MATCH(Part-(Includes)->IncludesPart)
                  --this joins the anchor to the recursive
                  --part of the query
                AND BaseRows.RelatedToPartNodeId = Part.$node_id
    )
SELECT PartName, SUM(IncludeCount) AS IncludeCountTotal
FROM BaseRows
WHERE BaseRows.PartName <> 'Shelvii'
  --filter out nonleaf nodes
  AND RelatedToPartNodeId NOT IN (SELECT $from_id
                                  FROM   PartsSystem.Includes)
GROUP BY PartName
ORDER BY PartName;
```

This returns

```
PartName                        IncludeCountTotal
------------------------------  -----------------
Flat Shelf                      5
Shelvii Shelf Enhancer          6
Shelvii Side                    2
Small Screw                     33
Wooden Dowel                    15
```

If you refer back to Figure 7-5, you will be able to reconcile to the number of items you expected.

Summary

In this chapter, you learned about some of the common types of issues you may have when building a directed acyclic graph that is not a tree. The code is very much the same base code as you have used over and over in the book, and for good reason. All the graph data structures based on the adjacency list structures behave similarly.

DAGs are very similar to tree structures because you typically work from parent to child in a structure to find data. In some ways, all DAGs work similarly, but in some uses where you need to see or calculate all row values, they behave quite different. Using SHORTEST_PATH can do some things (like interrogate what is in the DAG), but if you are not careful, queries can be lossy in ways that aren't completely obvious.

CHAPTER 8

A Graph For Testing

This is the final chapter. In it, you are going to see a reasonably simple, but common, graph example that you can use to explore how to query a cyclic graph. In the downloads, there is a code generator that will let you tune an example to your precise size needs and see what happens when the data amounts are tremendous.

This tool will let you dial in a graph size that you want to test on typical consumer hardware or a supercomputer. The example can be easily adapted for as large of a row set as you want to have.

Pretty much all of the techniques in this chapter were introduced in earlier chapters (especially Chapter 3), so none of it should be exactly new, but it should serve as both a refresher and a way to build your own test rig for testing performance.

The Example

For this model, I decided to keep it very simple. Just `Account`, `Follows`, `InterestedIn`, and `Interests`. Figure 8-1 shows the conceptual data mode for the model.

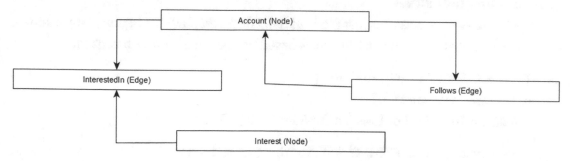

Figure 8-1. *Example conceptual model*

© Louis Davidson 2023
L. Davidson, *Practical Graph Structures in SQL Server and Azure SQL*,
https://doi.org/10.1007/978-1-4842-9459-8_8

Creating the Tables

The table design continues the minimalist approach, with only a single text column in each node to serve as the natural key value for you to work with. For account, it is the AccountHandle (which in the data is formatted as @ + Name.)

```
CREATE SCHEMA SocialGraph;
GO
CREATE TABLE SocialGraph.Account (
   AccountHandle nvarchar(30)
      CONSTRAINT AKAccount_Handle UNIQUE,
   --clusters on Node_id columns. Most fetches
   --will be on node_id, Handle usually only
   --when getting first row(s)
   CONSTRAINT PKAccount PRIMARY KEY ($node_id)
) AS NODE;
```

Note the PRIMARY KEY constraint on the $node_id pseudocolumn for this example. This is so that any lookups on the graph's internal keys will bring all the other columns along for the ride. There is a UNIQUE constraint on the AccountHandle column because 1, it needs to be unique and 2, you will be using it to lookup a row or two in almost every example.

Since the table is clustered on $node_id, the columns that make up that key will be in every row in that index as well, essentially making them both covering indexes for any query that uses the indexes.

The Follows edge contains just FollowTime. I don't display that in any of my queries (for space reasons), but you can filter rows based on the edge table columns too.

```
CREATE TABLE SocialGraph.Follows (
   FollowTime datetime2(0)
      CONSTRAINT DFLTFollows_FollowTime DEFAULT SYSDATETIME(),

      --cannot add a PRIMARY KEY to the $from_id and $to_id
      --columns because they allow NULL values. SO the UNIQUE
      --CLUSTERED index
   CONSTRAINT AKFollows_UniqueNodes UNIQUE CLUSTERED
                                  ( $to_id, $from_id),
      --same columns, in reverse for when you are fetching
```

```
        --by $to_id
        --like for fetching follower, not who you follow

        CONSTRAINT AKFollows_FromTO UNIQUE ( $from_id, $to_id),

        --just allow connections from Account to Account
        CONSTRAINT ECFollows_AccountToAccount
            CONNECTION (SocialGraph.Account TO
                    SocialGraph.Account) ON DELETE NO Action
) AS EDGE;
```

Next up is a trigger on the Follows edge to make sure you don't have any self-relationships. One of the times it is most important to have good constraints is when you are generating data for a test. I personally advocate for using them in all cases, but random data has a tendency to be slightly dirtier than user-generated data. (It is not always the case that self-relationships are bad, but in a follows relationship it is generally non-sensical.)

```
CREATE TRIGGER SocialGraph.Follows_IU_Trigger ON SocialGraph.Follows
AFTER INSERT, UPDATE
AS
BEGIN
    IF EXISTS (SELECT *
                FROM    inserted
                WHERE   $from_id = $to_id)
        BEGIN
         ROLLBACK;
         THROW 50000,'Modified data introduces a self reference',1;
        END;
END;
GO
```

Next, create the Interest and InterestedIn edges. They are configured very much like the other two objects (except when implementing a relationship between two nodes in different objects, you don't have to worry about that self-relationship):

```
CREATE TABLE SocialGraph.Interest (
    InterestName nvarchar(30)
```

```
        CONSTRAINT AKInterest_InterestName UNIQUE,
      CONSTRAINT PKInterest PRIMARY KEY ($node_id)
) AS NODE;

CREATE TABLE SocialGraph.InterestedIn
(
     CONSTRAINT AKInterestedIn_UniqueNodes
            UNIQUE CLUSTERED ($from_id, $to_id),
     CONSTRAINT AKInterestedIn_ToFrom UNIQUE ($to_id, $from_id),
     CONSTRAINT ECInterestedIn_AccountToInterestBoth
          CONNECTION (SocialGraph.Account TO SocialGraph.Interest)
                                   ON DELETE NO ACTION
)
AS EDGE;
```

In the Chapter 8 downloads, in the `0001 - Create Tables.sql` file, there are also a staging tables for accounts and interests. Then there are .SQL files to stage that data (100000 `Accounts` and 434 `Interests`.) Using these rows, you can tailor the size of your dataset to be pretty large, and you can easily add more accounts to the staging table and ramp the numbers way up. The loading files have `:SETVAR` commands that let you tailor the size of the dataset. You can get the same dataset for every execution if you use the same seed. (For more details on generating repeatable data set, this blog post I wrote covers it: `www.red-gate.com/simple-talk/blogs/generating-repeatable-sets-of-test-rows/`).

In the downloads at `https://github.com/drsqlgithub/GraphBook1`, sometime after publication, there will be tools to implement several other test datasets, including one that is based on the data from IMDB, if you want a truly large and real dataset. With millions and millions of nodes and connections, it can be a challenge to manage because of its size, but it is a fun dataset.

Loading the Data

In this section, I want to briefly explain how to load the random data. In the Chapter 8 downloads, there are two files that are used to load random data sets. Each of them has a number of `:SETVAR` commands to create SQLCMD variables. The first one loads the data into the table to implement the data like you see in Figure 8-2.

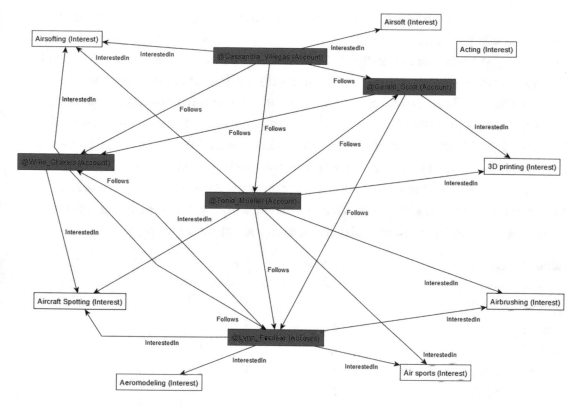

Figure 8-2. *Graph diagram for chapter's sample queries*

The darker shaded (or yellow if you have the eBook) nodes are the Account nodes, and the unshaded are Interest nodes (still unshaded in the eBook!). I generated this data using the following parameters:

```
:SETVAR SeedValue 259906607

--Max 100000
:SETVAR AccountCount 5
--Max 434
:SETVAR InterestCount 8

:SETVAR FollowsCount 20

:SETVAR MaxInterestPerAccount 8
```

If you use the same SeedValue and the same parameters, every time you run the queries in that file, you get the same output. If you change the values, you get different outcomes. I suggest that generally, if you are going to change values, change the seed value also. Otherwise, your data may include similarities that confuse you test to test.

In terms of follows and interests, the AccountCount and InterestCount values tune the number of nodes. The FollowsCount tells you how many Follows edge rows will be created, and MaxInterestPerAccount tunes how many Interests are possible per account. If that value is 10, then every account will have between 0 and 10 interests.

If you just execute the entire batch in the random data scripts, there are several bits of output that are useful to get a feel for the dataset. For example, one output is the following (I removed the $node_id column from the output for clarity):

AccountHandle	Froms	Tos
@Cassandra_Villegas	3	0
@Tonia_Mueller	2	1
@Gerald_Scott	2	2
@Lynn_Escobar	1	3
@Willie_Charles	1	3

This lets you see that there are three accounts where @Cassandra_Villegas is following other accounts (which makes it a nice anchor node for many of your queries). When I execute this query after loading the large random set, this is what the first five rows (of 100,000) looks like:

AccountHandle	Froms	Tos
@Bryant_Huber	10	10
@Sheila_Sherman	9	11
@Stacy_Charles	13	7
@Angelica_O'Neill	7	12
@Armando_Swanson	9	10

This makes for quite an interesting graph to process. The downloads include a set of parameters that I used for the non-performance testing sections of this chapter that have only the few accounts that match Figure 8-1.

The Queries

In the following sections, I go through a procession of queries that you will likely want to do on highly connected data in a cyclic graph. These are also the queries in the test rig that get executed to test the data structures with considerably larger amounts of data.

Find Every Node That Is Connected to a Specific Node

In Figure 8-1, you can see a couple of interesting relationships. @Cassandra_Villegas is connected directly to three other accounts and the other account node that exists through all the other paths. In the following query, you can see this:

```
--1 In Test Rig (corresponds to query in the test rig file that
--can be used to run all the queries using parameters you
--want to try out
        --item that the searched for item is connected to
SELECT  LAST_VALUE(Account2.AccountHandle)
           WITHIN GROUP (GRAPH PATH) AS ConnectedToAccountHandle,
        --how far away in structure
        COUNT(Account2.AccountHandle)
           WITHIN GROUP (GRAPH PATH) AS LEVEL,
     --what path was taken
        STRING_AGG(Account2.AccountHandle, '->')
              WITHIN GROUP (GRAPH PATH) AS ConnectedPath
FROM    SocialGraph.Account AS Account1
        ,SocialGraph.Account FOR PATH AS Account2
        ,SocialGraph.Follows FOR PATH AS Follows
WHERE   MATCH(SHORTEST_PATH(Account1(-(Follows)->Account2)+))
   AND  Account1.AccountHandle = '@Cassandra_Villegas'
ORDER BY ConnectedPath
OPTION (MAXDOP 1); --larger datasets can cause queries using
   --MATCH and especially SHORTEST_PATH to spin constantly
   --when parallellism occurs.
```

As you have seen in many results in the book so far, @Lynn_Escobar only shows up once because SHORTEST_PATH only gives you one path. Looking at Figure 8-2, there is more than one connection between the nodes.

```
ConnectedToAccountHandle   LEVEL   ConnectedPath
------------------------   ------   --------------------------------
@Gerald_Scott                 1     @Gerald_Scott
@Tonia_Mueller                1     @Tonia_Mueller
@Lynn_Escobar                 2     @Tonia_Mueller->@Lynn_Escobar
@Willie_Charles               1     @Willie_Charles
```

Later in the chapter I will demonstrate how to fetch all the paths, which is similar to how it was done in Chapter 7, but slightly different for a cyclical data structure. However, this will typically be useful more when you have two nodes you already know connect and now want to see what ways they connect.

For example, say @Cassandra_Villegas is trying to sell something to @Lynn_Escobar. If they don't want to go through @Tonia_Mueller for some reason, looking at all the paths might be useful. For very large graphs (especially when you aren't trying to see what your system can handle), it is a good idea to change the + in the MATCH(SHORTEST_PATH) condition to something smaller than everything. In a highly connected graph, you could easily be connected to almost everyone. (It would be interesting to see if everyone is connected to everyone else on LinkedIn, for example, certainly at 100 levels away.)

In almost every case, knowing that one user is connected to another by twenty or fifty node walks is of no realistic value in any scenario I can think of, even academically.

Note that I added OPTION (MAXDOP 1) to the query. This is one of the primary things you may need to do when tuning queries using SQL Server graph. Even in SQL Server 2022 there can be issues with performance when SHORTEST_PATH queries access a lot of rows. Obviously, in the first half of this chapter, the data sizes are small, but when you try queries that access larger numbers of rows (a script to load this schema with considerable amounts of data is included in the download), some queries can run for 24 hours and not make progress without MAXDOP 1.

Of all the advice provided in the book, this tip is something to check on if you are using a version later than SQL Server 2022.

Seeing If One Node is Connected to Another

In the next query, let's first explore that question of filtering your query to see if two nodes connect. The most typical way is to use a CTE to represent all connections to the account and then filter it in the CTE:

```
--2 in test rig
WITH BaseRows AS (
SELECT Account1.AccountHandle + '->' +
        STRING_AGG(Account2.AccountHandle, '->')
          WITHIN GROUP (GRAPH PATH) AS ConnectedPath,
        LAST_VALUE(Account2.AccountHandle)
          WITHIN GROUP (GRAPH PATH) AS ConnectedToAccountHandle,
        COUNT(Account2.AccountHandle)
          WITHIN GROUP (GRAPH PATH) AS Level
FROM    SocialGraph.Account AS Account1
        ,SocialGraph.Account FOR PATH AS Account2
        ,SocialGraph.Follows FOR PATH AS Follows
WHERE   MATCH(SHORTEST_PATH(Account1(-(Follows)->Account2)+))
  --starting point
  AND   Account1.AccountHandle = '@Cassandra_Villegas'
)
SELECT *
FROM    BaseRows
        --is the starting point connected to:
WHERE   ConnectedToAccountHandle = '@Lynn_Escobar'
OPTION (MAXDOP 1);
```

This returns the following. (I only output the ConnectedPath in the book, even when there are more columns just for formatting sake. Everything in the rest of the output can be visually extrapolated from the path.)

```
ConnectedPath
----------------------------------------------------
@Cassandra_Villegas->@Tonia_Mueller->@Lynn_Escobar
```

In some cases, I have found that filtering in the query itself can be troublesome. So, it can be useful to just save off the contents of the baserows into a temp table like this:

```
DROP TABLE IF EXISTS #hold
--3 in test rig
SELECT Account1.AccountHandle + '->' +
        STRING_AGG(Account2.AccountHandle, '->')
            WITHIN GROUP (GRAPH PATH) AS ConnectedPath,
        LAST_VALUE(Account2.AccountHandle)
            WITHIN GROUP (GRAPH PATH) AS ConnectedToAccountHandle,
        COUNT(Account2.AccountHandle)
            WITHIN GROUP (GRAPH PATH) AS Level
INTO #hold
FROM    SocialGraph.Account AS Account1
        ,SocialGraph.Account FOR PATH AS Account2
        ,SocialGraph.Follows FOR PATH AS Follows
WHERE   MATCH(SHORTEST_PATH(Account1(-(Follows)->Account2)+))
  AND   Account1.AccountHandle = '@Cassandra_Villegas'
ORDER BY ConnectedPath
OPTION (MAXDOP 1);

SELECT *
FROM    #hold
WHERE   ConnectedToAccountHandle = '@Lynn_Escobar';
```

This has the same output and may have the same performance as the CTE. But like any SQL queries, when the data sizes get very large, it can help to give the optimizer a hand and split the queries up.

Both versions of this query appear in the test rig to compare the performance of them both.

Returning All Paths Between Two Nodes

While it is often useful just to know that you are connected to a person, it may also be interesting to know the multiple ways you are connected. There are a few ways of doing this.

For example, for the first two levels, you can write two SELECT statements. One is for the direct connections. The other is for second level connections. UNION them together and you can see two levels of connection.

```
--4
SELECT   1 AS Level, '' AS ConnectedThrough, Account2.AccountHandle
FROM     SocialGraph.Account AS Account1,
         SocialGraph.Follows,
             SocialGraph.Account AS Account2
WHERE    MATCH(Account1-(Follows)->Account2)
  AND    Account1.AccountHandle = '@Cassandra_Villegas'
  AND    Account2.AccountHandle = '@Lynn_Escobar'
UNION ALL
SELECT   2 AS Level, Account2.AccountHandle AS ConnectedThrough, Account3.
AccountHandle
FROM     SocialGraph.Account AS Account1,
         SocialGraph.Follows,
             SocialGraph.Account AS Account2,
         SocialGraph.Follows AS Follows2,
             SocialGraph.Account AS Account3
WHERE    MATCH(Account1-(Follows)->Account2-(Follows2)->Account3)
  AND    Account1.AccountHandle = '@Cassandra_Villegas'
  AND    Account3.AccountHandle = '@Lynn_Escobar'
ORDER BY AccountHandle;
```

This returns

Level	ConnectedThrough	AccountHandle
2	@Tonia_Mueller	@Lynn_Escobar
2	@Willie_Charles	@Lynn_Escobar
2	@Gerald_Scott	@Lynn_Escobar

There are no one-level connections between @Cassandra_Villegas and @Lynn_Escobar, but there are three two-level connections.

On the one hand, this is quite tedious to write, particularly if you need to do this many more levels. On the other hand, this probably will perform quite nicely because it really is just a few joins through the edge. I didn't opt to test for 10-20 level paths because it is so tedious to write.

If you want to see **all** paths for **all** levels, you need to use a recursive CTE. It is a fairly essential skill because generally you may need to see all the paths between two nodes, which was something you also needed in the previous chapter with the DAG implementation of a bill of materials.

The biggest difference between earlier examples is that you are dealing with a cyclical structure. The thing you must add to the recursive query is to stop the recursion when you hit any cycles in the output. Back in Figure 8-1, you can see that @Willie_Charles and @Lynn_Escobar follow each other.

Note that this was also covered back in Chapter 3, but I am including here again because it fits and you will want to test it with this dataset.

You can write the following query, filtering for the one account where you want to see how they connect. I also limited the output to five levels:

```
--Getting the same answer as the last example
--5 in test rig
DECLARE @MaxLevel int =5,
           @AccountHandle nvarchar(30) = '@Cassandra_Villegas',
           @DetermineHowConnected nvarchar(30) =
                                         '@Lynn_Escobar';

WITH BaseRows
AS (
    --the CTE anchor is just the starting node
    SELECT Account.AccountHandle AS AccountHandle,
           Account.AccountHandle AS FollowsAccountHandle,

        --the path that contains the readable path we have
        --built in all examples with the anchor included
          CAST('\' + Account.AccountHandle + '\'
                                         AS nvarchar(4000)) AS Path,
          0 AS level -the level
    FROM SocialGraph.Account
    WHERE Account.AccountHandle = @AccountHandle
    UNION ALL
```

```
--pretty typical 1 level graph query:
SELECT  Account.AccountHandle,
        FollowedAccount.AccountHandle
                    AS FollowsAccountHandle,
        BaseRows.Path + FollowedAccount.AccountHandle + '\',
        BaseRows.level + 1
FROM SocialGraph.Account,
        SocialGraph.Follows,
        SocialGraph.Account AS FollowedAccount,
        BaseRows
WHERE MATCH(Account-(Follows)->FollowedAccount)
    --this joins the anchor to the recursive
      --part of the query
    AND BaseRows.FollowsAccountHandle =
                                    Account.AccountHandle
--this is the part that stops recursion, treating the
    --string value like an array
    AND NOT BaseRows.Path LIKE CONCAT('%\',
                        FollowedAccount.AccountHandle, '\%')
            AND BaseRows.level < @MaxLevel
)
SELECT Path —for space reasons only
FROM BaseRows
WHERE FollowsAccountHandle = @DetermineHowConnected
ORDER BY Path;
```

Executing this code returns the following results:

```
Path
\@Cassandra_Villegas\@Gerald_Scott\@Lynn_Escobar\
\@Cassandra_Villegas\@Gerald_Scott\@Willie_Charles\@Lynn_Escobar\
\@Cassandra_Villegas\@Tonia_Mueller\@Gerald_Scott\@Lynn_Escobar\
\@Cassandra_Villegas\@Tonia_Mueller\@Gerald_Scott\@Willie_Charles
                                                    \@Lynn_Escobar\
\@Cassandra_Villegas\@Tonia_Mueller\@Lynn_Escobar\
\@Cassandra_Villegas\@Willie_Charles\@Lynn_Escobar\
```

You can see that in the results, there are three rows that are two hops away, which matches the previous result in the UNION query, but there are also a few more walks from the row you searched for and the row you are matching to.

From there you could filter/sort the output using the level or the path. For example, change the previous query's where clause to include

```
AND Path like '_%\@Tonia_Mueller\%_'
```

Now the query gets only paths that pass through @Tonia_Mueller.

The part of the code that stops the recursion is

```
        AND NOT BaseRows.Path LIKE CONCAT('%\',
                        FollowedAccount.AccountHandle, '\%')
```

It does this by comparing the current path in the loop to a LIKE expression. That LIKE expression takes the current node in the query and surrounds it with characters so that if it is in the path, you can stop processing. So, if the path is '\1\2\' and the next node is 3, you get '\1\2\3\' LIKE '%\3\%'. This is one of the limitations of a relational database: no arrays (and this is one of the only places I have ever thought that an array would be useful). I know other RDBMSs have them, but I expect they are problematic in most of their usage.

The lack of the array means you will use the data in the string as a delimited list and see if the current node is in that path already.

Finding All People That a User Connects To At Any Level Where They Share an Interest

Where the graph syntax really starts to shine is finding even more connections though even more nodes. In this case, you want to find users connected to each other at any level that have an interest in Aircraft Spotting. Cassandra does not currently have this interest noted, but it doesn't matter if they do in this particular example. The idea here might be that Cassandra is interested in taking up Aircraft Spotting and wants to see if any connections already do this.

To implement this, use LAST_NODE to get the last node in the chain and then match these nodes to their interests to see if Aircraft Spotting is included:

```
--6 in test rig
----any level connection and connections have a specific interest
```

```
SELECT Account1.AccountHandle + '->' +
        STRING_AGG(Account2.AccountHandle, '->')
            WITHIN GROUP (GRAPH PATH) AS ConnectedPath,
        LAST_VALUE(Account2.AccountHandle)
            WITHIN GROUP (GRAPH PATH) AS ConnectedToAccountHandle,
        COUNT(Account2.AccountHandle)
            WITHIN GROUP (GRAPH PATH) AS LEVEL,
        Interest.InterestName
FROM    SocialGraph.Account AS Account1
        ,SocialGraph.Account FOR PATH AS Account2
        ,SocialGraph.Follows FOR PATH AS Follows
        ,SocialGraph.InterestedIn
        ,SocialGraph.Interest
--This finds people that the searched for person follows
WHERE   MATCH(SHORTEST_PATH(Account1(-(Follows)->Account2)+)
    --and this takes every matched node (the last node in the chain
    --and sees if they are connected to Interest
    AND LAST_NODE(Account2)-(InterestedIn)->Interest)
    --The next two lines filter the results;
    AND   Account1.AccountHandle = '@Cassandra_Villegas'
    AND   Interest.InterestName = 'Aircraft Spotting'
ORDER BY ConnectedPath
OPTION (MAXDOP 1);
```

This returns (including only the path for space reasons)

```
ConnectedPath
----------------------------------------------------------
@Cassandra_Villegas->@Tonia_Mueller
@Cassandra_Villegas->@Tonia_Mueller->@Lynn_Escobar
@Cassandra_Villegas->@Willie_Charles
```

Trace the connections on Figure 8-2 and you will see these three people share an affinity for Aircraft Spotting and are all followed by @Cassandra_Villegas. These kind of queries are where people like marketers can start to hone the types of sets that let them entice you with products from people like you, or that you like, and share interests or purchases, maybe matching what you have searched for.

These kinds of queries won't typically go very deep into the structure because the farther away from the anchor node, the less interesting the suggestions would be. (Who hasn't gotten a suggestion on Amazon for a product that "people like you" purchased that caused you to scratch your head.)

Finding a Specific User Who a User Connects To at Any Level Where They Share a Specific Interest

This next query is very similar but also very different. This time the LAST_NODE expression requires that the notes share an interest:

```
WHERE  MATCH(SHORTEST_PATH(Account1(-(Follows)->Account2)+)
  --Both Accounts interested in the same thing
  AND LAST_NODE(Account2)-(InterestedIn)->Interest
                                <-(InterestedIn2)-Account1)
  AND   Account1.AccountHandle = '@Cassandra_Villegas'
```

The MATCH expression is the same, so you are looking for accounts that follow each other on any level. Now you take the last node and do a connection from the last node account to the account that is the anchor through Interest:

```
--8 in test rig
--any level connection and shared common interest
WITH BaseRows AS (
SELECT Account1.AccountHandle + '->' +
        STRING_AGG(Account2.AccountHandle, '->')
            WITHIN GROUP (GRAPH PATH) AS ConnectedPath,
        LAST_VALUE(Account2.AccountHandle)
            WITHIN GROUP (GRAPH PATH) AS ConnectedToAccountHandle,
        COUNT(Account2.AccountHandle)
            WITHIN GROUP (GRAPH PATH) AS LEVEL,
        Interest.InterestName AS InterestName
FROM    SocialGraph.Account AS Account1
        ,SocialGraph.Account FOR PATH AS Account2
        ,SocialGraph.Follows FOR PATH AS Follows
        ,SocialGraph.InterestedIn
        ,SocialGraph.InterestedIn AS InterestedIn2
```

```
                ,SocialGraph.Interest
WHERE   MATCH(SHORTEST_PATH(Account1(-(Follows)->Account2)+)
    --Both Accounts interested in the same thing
    AND LAST_NODE(Account2)-(InterestedIn)->Interest
                            <-(InterestedIn2)-Account1)
    AND   Account1.AccountHandle = '@Cassandra_Villegas'
)
SELECT InterestName, ConnectedPath
FROM    BaseRows
WHERE   ConnectedToAccountHandle = '@Tonia_Mueller'
ORDER BY ConnectedPath
OPTION (MAXDOP 1);
```

Filtering the output for @Tonia_Mueller, this returns only

```
InterestName   ConnectedPath
-------------  --------------------------------------------
Airsofting     @Cassandra_Villegas->@Tonia_Mueller
```

which tells us that they are connected by following and share an interest. You can see this clearly in Figure 8-2.

If you want to filter the InterestName value and see what accounts are followed on any level for an interest, you just need to filter that in the WHERE clause, which you can do because the edge found in the LAST_NODE expression is not declared as being FOR PATH. The following snippet comes from the CTE in the previous query:

```
WHERE   MATCH(SHORTEST_PATH(Account1(-(Follows)->Account2)+)
AND LAST_NODE(Account2)-(InterestedIn)->Interest
                                <-(InterestedIn2)-Account1)
AND   Account1.AccountHandle = '@Cassandra_Villegas'
AND   Interest.InterestName =  'Airsofting'
```

The full query, when executed, has the same output for the previous query: two rows. If you remove the WHERE clause from the outer query, no longer limiting the output to @Tonia_Mueller, then you will see that @Willie_Charles also shares the same interest. (Note that example is number 9 in the test rig and example queries.)

```
ConnectedPath
-----------------------------------------
@Cassandra_Villegas->@Tonia_Mueller
@Cassandra_Villegas->@Willie_Charles
```

Finding Connections Through Other Nodes

In these last set of query examples, you are going to do one of the more interesting types of queries you will want to do with your graphs, that of connecting nodes though relationships with different nodes.

For example, in the graph, instead of following connections through the Follows edge, let's consider them connected when they share an interest. This first query gives you first-level connections through Airsofting:

```
--10 in test rig
SELECT  Account1.AccountHandle,
        Interest.InterestName,
        Account2.AccountHandle
FROM    SocialGraph.Account AS Account1
        ,SocialGraph.Account AS Account2
        ,SocialGraph.InterestedIn AS InterestedIn1
        ,SocialGraph.InterestedIn  AS InterestedIn2
        ,SocialGraph.Interest AS Interest
WHERE   MATCH(Account1-(InterestedIn1)->Interest
                               <-(InterestedIn2)-Account2)
  AND   Account1.AccountHandle = '@Cassandra_Villegas'
  AND   Account1.AccountHandle <> Account2.AccountHandle
  AND   Interest.InterestName = 'Airsofting'
OPTION (MAXDOP 1);
```

This gives you the first-level connections through edges connecting to Airsofting. This result isn't surprising, and you have done this same before one level away.

```
AccountHandle            InterestName    AccountHandle
--------------------     -------------   -----------------------
@Cassandra_Villegas      Airsofting      @Tonia_Mueller
@Cassandra_Villegas      Airsofting      @Willie_Charles
```

Casandra connects to Tonia and Willie through a shared interest in Airsofting. But now what interests do Tonia and Willie share with others? Well, it turns out that you can use SHORTEST_PATH over these more complex MATCH expressions as well:

```
--11 in test rig
SELECT Account1.AccountHandle
+ '->' +
        STRING_AGG(CONCAT('(',Interest.InterestName,')->',
                                Account2.AccountHandle) , '->')
          WITHIN GROUP (GRAPH PATH) AS ConnectedPath,
        LAST_VALUE(Account2.AccountHandle)
          WITHIN GROUP (GRAPH PATH) AS ConnectedToAccountHandle,
        COUNT(Account2.AccountHandle)
          WITHIN GROUP (GRAPH PATH) AS Level
FROM    SocialGraph.Account AS Account1
        ,SocialGraph.Account FOR PATH AS Account2
        ,SocialGraph.InterestedIn FOR PATH AS InterestedIn1
        ,SocialGraph.InterestedIn FOR PATH AS InterestedIn2
        ,SocialGraph.Interest FOR PATH AS Interest
        --only fetching 2 levels for testing reasons. This
        --is where tests can get bogged down, so keeping it to
        --only what you want/need is important
WHERE   MATCH(SHORTEST_PATH(Account1(-(InterestedIn1)->Interest
                                <-(InterestedIn2)-Account2){1,2}))
  AND   Account1.AccountHandle = '@Cassandra_Villegas'
OPTION (MAXDOP 1);
GO
```

This returns the following paths:

```
ConnectedPath
----------------------------------------------------------------
@Cassandra_Villegas->(Airsofting)->@Tonia_Mueller
@Cassandra_Villegas->(Airsofting)->@Cassandra_Villegas
@Cassandra_Villegas->(Airsofting)->@Willie_Charles
```

```
@Cassandra_Villegas->(Airsofting)->@Tonia_Mueller->(3D printing)
                                              ->@Gerald_Scott
@Cassandra_Villegas->(Airsofting)->@Tonia_Mueller->(Air sports)
                                              ->@Lynn_Escobar
```

This type of solution doesn't make as much sense in a model like this. One-level connection on the same interest does, but the second-level value starts to fade unless the interests share a commonality that you did not include in the model. You probably want to filter to a category of interest. To do that, you need to use a CTE/derived table here:

```
,SocialGraph.Interest FOR PATH AS Interest
```

And use

```
(SELECT *
   FROM SocialGraph.Interest
   WHERE InterestType IN ('Something','SomethingElse') as Interest
```

Where this can be useful is if you have a database like the IMDB database. If you want to see who worked with whom, you may have to go one or more edges that show that one person worked on a piece of work in some capacity (and you might want to limit the connection to type of work, like TV, Movie, or even Genre of Horror, Comedy, etc.). You don't have a direct connection from person to person, but you do have this indirect connection indicating a shared experience.

Beware, however, that when you do this type of query, you are creating a type of non-directed graph that you are processing, because if Node1 shares an interest with Node2, it follows that Node2 shares an interest with Node1. This will make the breadth-first processing blow up quickly so it is best to limit this output to a reasonable number of hops if your node and edge counts are high.

Performance Tuning Results

In the downloads, I included files named 0010 Load Large Random Data Set.sql and 0011 - Test Rig (Queries With Timing Capture.sql. Assuming you have been following along and building the tables and have loaded the staging tables, these two files will load a pretty large test data set and run a bank of queries against that same data set. (If you haven't been following along, there are files to create and load the objects in the same chapter directory.)

As I stated back when I did the tree performance testing, my test server was bought from Amazon with the description Intel NUC 9 NUC9i7QNX (Intel 6-Core i7-9750H, 64GB RAM, 2TB PCIe SSD, 2 x Thunderbolt, WiFi 6, HDMI, Win 10 Pro) Ghost Skull Canyon Extreme Gaming Box Elite). It's not a server class machine, but it is a solid machine for testing.

In the test rig, there are parameter values configured that will allow you to run the same queries. Table 8-1 shows the output of that batch. As you can see, most of the queries are very fast, but there is a major exception. Note that each row corresponds to the queries and sections in this chapter. The accounts chosen were just randomly chosen but are documented/changeable in the test rig download.

Table 8-1. *Test Results*

TestSetName	TimeDifferenceSeconds	RowsAffectedCount
1. Simple find all descendants	3	94162
2. Simple find specific descendant using where clause	1	1
3. Simple find specific descendant using temptable	2	1
4. Find two level connections just using MATCH	0	1
5. Find all paths between descendants using Follows, recursive	9	5
6. Any level follow and followers have specific interest	2	1518
7. Any level follow and followers have specific interest, temptable	6	1518
8. Any level follow and shared interest, CTE	1	1
9. Any level connection and shared specific interest	4	1489

(continued)

Table 8-1. (*continued*)

TestSetName	TimeDifferenceSeconds	RowsAffectedCount
10. Finding users that a person is connected to directly through specific interest	0	1582
11. Connection path through interest, starting with low cardinality, two levels	1163	93325
11a. Connection path through interest, a bit higher cardinality, 10 levels	2284	93325

Even returning 93 thousand rows and 12 levels deep, the query to find every rows that the anchor account was related to took only 3 seconds. Pretty much all of the queries performed adequately enough for me to take this solution to production (ideally with about half as many rows as I am testing with!).

The only outlier is the connecting though interest instead of the Follows relationship. Doing the SHORTEST_PATH through another node is definitely costly, not because the construct itself is so bad but, as previously noted, will be more likely to really blow up the number of rows processed. Doing this operation with a high cardinality relationship is costly.

What was really interesting in that query is that when I cranked it from 2 levels to 10, it took twice as long and returned exactly the same number of rows, so it didn't actually find any level three rows. (If there were actually 10 levels and the number of matches continued to grow, it could take a few months to complete.) I attempted to rewrite this in multiple ways, and each time it took a long time to execute. There were about 18,000 level-one rows with the parameters I chose. That initial first level fetch was very fast. When I tried to do the second pass on its own (which is basically to do all 18,000 rows at once), it took a long enough time that it wasn't worth including.

Of course, the intermediate set would likely be something like 18000 X 18000 in this very random data set, which is a lot of rows, and considering my CPUs are just mobile class CPUs, I have been mostly impressed with all I have experienced.

While official updates to the downloads will be on the Apress GitHub repo at `https://github.com/Apress/practical-graph-structures`, unofficial updates will be made in my corresponding GitHub repository here: `https://github.com/drsqlgithub/GraphBook1`. I will also share new graph techniques via my blog: `www.red-gate.com/simple-talk/author/louis-davidson/`.

Performance Tuning Roundup

The book has been peppered with tips about tuning your queries when using SQL Graph objects in SQL Server 2022 (and SQL Server 2019, since they are very similar internally, and the same syntactically). In this section, I want to review all of the tips I shared one last time before getting to the end of the book.

Test

The most obvious tip I can share is to test, test, test, before you get to production. With reasonably small amounts of data, queries on the SQL Graph objects are extremely fast. As I showed in the previous section, even on a limited server, most typical queries are very fast, even when they return a lot of rows. With 100,000 accounts, it took just seconds to connect nearly all those accounts 12 levels deep. But there are a few gotchas that are not easy to identify (even when you follow the rest of the advice in these sections).

By loading your tables with a lot more data that your users ever will, and running all the queries that users might, you can avoid some situations that can be devastating for performance.

Index the Internal Columns

Though the general advice with indexes is to be careful about adding too many, for the SQL Graph objects, don't be shy with them to a certain level (like don't apply the same index multiple times or anything!) While the pseudocolumns seem kind of mysterious, at least initially, they are not indexed by default to handle the most common operations you may execute. As a reminder, they represent a 4-byte integer (the `object_id` of the table) and an 8-byte integer value (the internal graph surrogate key value).

There are a few internal indexes on the objects when you create your node and edge objects, but they are not usually enough. None of the internal indexes are clustered indexes, so as you are testing your queries, consider what path you use commonly and index accordingly.

Consider using `INCLUDE` on some of your indexes that use the pseudocolumns when you can't cluster the indexes to avoid bookmark lookups. I didn't spend any time on the query plans because they are currently indecipherable in comparison to query plans on relational objects (the plans look linear, but as I have covered, the algorithms are actually iterative/recursive and do not map well to the current query plan format). But indexes on the `$to_id` (and `$from_id` for non-tree objects) are essential for getting the most out of your queries.

You can also index the `$node_id` on node objects, and even cluster on it depending on how your data is being accessed. The key is to think about how you are using your objects and adjust accordingly (and test it out, of course).

Employ a Maximum Degree of Parallelism of One

One of the strangest things that is required to optimize SQL Graph queries is to eliminate parallelism when a lot of data is involved. Why this wasn't just set as a default for SQL Graph queries in SQL Server 2022, I am not sure. But in my testing, I often had queries running 24 hours later and making no notable progress other than making my test computer's fans sweat. With `OPTION (MAXDOP 1)` set, the query might take 20 seconds or 20 minutes but finish in a time worth waiting for. It isn't a perfect solution, because on occasion you may still run into queries that take many, many hours and not seem to finish.

Consider Breaking Up Some Queries

A piece of general SQL Server tuning advice is that when queries take a long time and you can't figure out why, try rewriting them some way to make them work as you wish. This will help you find your performance issues, and on slightly rare occasions, it will be the best solution anyhow.

Find sections of the code that you can get to execute quickly and save results into a temporary table. Sometimes you may need to save off millions of rows over and over, but once you get data saved off into a temp table, you may find that the query is much faster. Sometimes it might seem like a lot of data to save off, but SQL Server's engine may actually be doing the same thing anyhow.

Earlier in this chapter, I included examples when I moved filtering from the main query to a temp table. In my most recent examples, it hasn't really changed the performance much; in fact, it was a tiny bit slower in some of these examples. But if the base query starts to fail in performance, you can break it down into sections and try to optimize the query.

Writing a query optimizer is a very complex thing and optimizing for every case that a user may think of can be complex. On the good side, though, most of the queries you would use in a typical OLTP system will not require traversing many levels of the structure. The less data you need to access, the more complex the queries can be without it being complicated.

And most queries in a data warehouse can be either waited on, or you can use something like the helper objects introduced in Chapter 6.

The End (or Is It the Beginning?)

While I may not have covered everything you will want to do with a graph, as there are many different uses you will have for a graph that I could not imagine, it is all I will cover in this edition of the book.

Microsoft SQL Server has had a graph implementation for five years now, and it is improving incrementally each edition. SQL Server 2022 had no outward indication of differences, but I understand there were some internal changes (though no indication of what they might be, or if there will be more in the future.)

There are many limitations to the product right now. There are still things like having to use MAXDOP 1 when using very large data sets that do plague the implementation today. There are a lot of limitations to the syntax, which I have mentioned, and if you don't remember them now, you will once you start coding.

SQL Server's graph implementation is not ready to be a replacement for purely graph databases, but it is a very nice extension to one of the best relational engines to help you extend your databases with graph elements, for example when a simple many-to-many relationship won't do, or if you want to look at all the many connections between your data, often by transforming relational tables into graph tables for analysts.

Index

A

Acyclic, 13, 19
Acyclic graphs, 164
    adjacency list, 27
    breadth-first algorithm, 19–21
    example, 19, 28
    polyhierarchy, 29
    sample graph, 22
    trees, 22, 23, 25–27
AdventureWorksLT, 87

B

Binary tree (simple tree), 25
Breadth-first algorithm, 19–21, 27, 29, 68,
    109, 164

C

Customer relationship management
    (CRM) system, 97
Cycle, 13
Cyclic, 19
Cyclic graphs, 37
    node-to-node relationships, 30
    non-directed, 35, 36
    product or product, customer, 31
    sales system, 31
    sample graph, 32, 33
    shortest path, 34
    weighted nodes, 34, 35

D

Data structure
    acyclic graphs, 19
    cyclic graphs, 30
    implementation, 17–19
DELETE operation, 84, 102, 141
Depth-first algorithm, 20
Directed acyclic graphs (DAG), 39, 121
    determining part, build, 197–199
    fictional Shelvii shelf system,
        194, 196, 197
    picklist query, 200
    printing out parts list, build, 201–206
    SHORTEST_PATH, 191–193, 207
Directed edge, 11
    directed graph, 11
    disconnected graph, 10
    isomorphic graph, 7
    NULL graph, 5
drsqlgithub repository, 166

E, F

Edge constraint, 101–107

G

Graph data structure
    applied math, 3
    bridge edges, 11
    computing/directed graphs, 11, 12

© Louis Davidson 2023
L. Davidson, *Practical Graph Structures in SQL Server and Azure SQL*,
https://doi.org/10.1007/978-1-4842-9459-8

Graph data structure (*cont.*)
    connected/disconnected graphs, 10
    cyclic/acyclic graphs, 13, 15
    database, 4
    definition, 1
    directed graph, 11
    disconnected graph, 10
    edge, 4–6
    Euler Walk, 9
    examples, 1
    graph objects, 2
    identical graph structures, 7
    isomorphic graph, 7
    many-to-many relationships, 1
    mathematical proofs, 2
    node, 4
    NULL graph, 5
    pure math, 3
    SQL, 4
    subgraph, 8

H

HASH JOIN operator, 82
Helper table
    data processing, 175
    denormalization, 175
    hierarchy display, 182, 183
    Kimball, 176–178, 180–182
    objects, 183–185
    performance, 186–189

I

Integrity constraints
    additional constraint, 111, 113–115
    edge, 101–104, 106, 107
    uniqueness, 107–110

J, K

JOIN operators, 48

L

LAST_NODE graph function, 75
LIKE expression, 222

M

MATCH expression, 48, 49, 51, 53, 55,
    57–59, 61, 65, 75, 81, 100, 113, 201,
    224, 227
Metadata, 115

N

NODE_ID_FROM_PARTS function, 89, 93

O

Online transaction processing system
    (OLTP) system, 127, 176, 233

P

Path, 8
Path technique
    code
        check child, 172
        CompanyId column, 168
        create script, 169
        insert new rows, 169
        report sales, 173, 174
        returning hierarchy, 170, 171
    LIKE expression, 167
    reparenting, 168
    sample graph, 166

Polyhierarchy, 15, 29, 191, 192
PRIMARY KEY constraint, 110, 210

Q

Querying data, SQL
    node-to-node querying
        ANSI join syntax, 51
        filter output, 51, 52
        FROM clause, 50
        MATCH expression, 48, 49
        multiple MATCH expression,
           53–55, 57, 58
        traversing variable level paths (*see*
           SHORTEST_PATH clause)

R

Relational recursion, 19
REPLACE function, 168

S

SELECT statements,
      46, 77, 92, 105, 218
SETVAR commands, 212
SHORTEST_PATH clause
    aggregates, 62, 64, 65
    checking connection, matched
        item, 73–75
    controlling depth, processing, 65–67
    displaying last node, 60–62
    filters, 67
    finding paths between nodes, 68, 70
    MATCH expression, 59
    weighted graph calculations, 71, 72
SQL Graph/adjacency list
      method, 165

SQL Server's graph tables
    heterogenous queries, 94–98, 100, 101
    integrity constraints, 101
    interface layer, 78
        creating edge, 78
        delete operations, 84–86
        insert, 78–84
        JSON tags, 87, 89, 91–93
    matadata
        graph columns, types, 116, 117
        graph information tools, 117, 118
        heterogenous queries, 119
        list graph objects, 115
STRING_AGG function, 63
Subgraph, 8, 65, 155, 176, 177, 203, 204

T

Tabular data stream (TDS), 97
Testing performance, graph
    conceptual data mode, 209
    creating tables, 210–212
    data warehouse, 233
    implementation, 233
    index internal columns, 232
    loading data, 212–214
    parallelism, 232
    performance tuning
        results, 228–230
    queries
        connecting nodes, 226–228
        node connection, 215, 216
        returning path between two
          nodes, 218–221
        shares interest, 224, 225
        two nodes connect, 217, 218
    test, 231
Transitive closure, 14

Tree data structures, 22
    aggregating, 154
    balanced, 26
    base table
        structure, 122–125
    creating new nodes, 128–137
    deleting nodes, 141–148
    orders of magnitude, 162
    output code
        aggregating child activity, 154–158,
          160, 161
        child node exists, 151, 152
        procedures, 149
        return part, 149, 150
    real code, 127
    reparenting nodes, 138–140
    sales data, 125–127

    set of objects, 122
    SQL Graph objects, xvi
    shallow, 27
TRY CATCH blocks, 127
T-SQL language
    creating data, 43–47
    object creation, 40–43

U, V

UNION ALL operators, 46
Uniqueness constraints, 24, 87, 107–111,
    119, 123

W, X, Y, Z

Walk, 8

Printed in the United States
by Baker & Taylor Publisher Services